Table of Contents

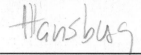

Hansburg

Table of Contents *continued*

Introduction

The National Council of Teachers of English and the International Reading Association prepared standards for the English language arts. These standards "grew out of current research and theory about how students learn—in particular, how they learn language." These standards address "what students should know and be able to do in the English language arts."

One standard is that students should be able to communicate effectively by learning the "language of wider communication," the forms of the English language that are most commonly identified as standard English. Students must recognize the importance of audience when they write and speak so they will be able to use the appropriate form of language for the intended audience. The standards acknowledge that "students need guidance and practice to develop their skills in academic writing. . . . They need to understand the varying demands of different kinds of writing tasks and to recognize how to adapt tone, style, and content for the particular task at hand." Again, students must "consider the needs of their audiences as they compose, edit, and revise."

Another standard emphasizes that "students apply knowledge of language structure, language conventions. . . ." Students need practice with accepted language conventions (e.g., capitalization, punctuation, grammar) in order to develop awareness and consistent application in their writing.

Language Practice is a program designed for students who require additional practice in the basics of effective writing and speaking. Focused practice in key grammar, usage, mechanics, and composition areas helps students gain ownership of essential skills. The logical sequence of the practice exercises, combined with a clear and concise format, allows for easy and independent use.

National Council of Teachers of English and International Reading Association, *Standards for the English Language Arts*, 1996.

Organization

Language Practice provides systematic, focused attention to just one carefully selected skill at a time. Rules are clearly stated at the beginning of each lesson. Key terms are introduced in bold type. The rules are then illustrated with examples and followed by meaningful practice exercises.

Lessons are organized around a series of units. They are arranged in a logical sequence beginning with vocabulary; progressing through sentences, grammar and usage, and mechanics; and culminating with composition skills.

Grades 3 through 8 include a final unit on study skills, which can be assigned as needed. This unit includes such skills as organizing information, following directions, using a dictionary, using the library, and choosing appropriate reference sources.

Skills are reviewed thoroughly in a two-page test at the conclusion of each unit. These unit tests are presented in a standardized test format. The content of each unit is repeated and expanded in subsequent levels as highlighted in the skills correlation chart on pages 6 and 7.

Use

Throughout the program, *Language Practice* stresses the application of language principles. In addition to matching, circling, or underlining elements in a predetermined sentence, lessons ask students to use what they have learned in an original sentence or in rewriting a sentence.

Language Practice is designed for independent use by students who have had instruction in the specific skills covered in these lessons. Copies of the activities can be given to individuals, pairs of students, or small groups for completion. They can also be used as a center activity. If students are familiar with the content, the worksheets can be homework for reviewing and reinforcing skills.

From the beginning, students feel comfortable with the format of the lessons. Each lesson is introduced with a rule at the top of the page and ends with a meaningful exercise at the bottom of the page. Each lesson is clearly labeled, and directions are clear and uncomplicated. Because the format is logical and consistent and the vocabulary is carefully controlled, most students can use *Language Practice* with a high degree of independence. As the teacher, this allows you the time needed to help students on a one-to-one basis.

Special Feature

The process approach to teaching writing provides success for most students. *Language Practice* provides direct support for the teaching of composition and significantly enhances those strategies and techniques commonly associated with the process-writing approach.

Each book includes a composition unit that provides substantial work with important composition skills, such as considering audience, writing topic sentences, selecting supporting details, taking notes, writing reports, and revising and proofreading. Also included in the composition unit is practice with various prewriting activities, such as clustering and brainstorming, which play an important role in process writing. The composition lessons are presented in the same rule-plus-practice format as in other units.

Additional Notes

- Parent Communication. Sign the *Letter to Parents* and send it home with the students. This letter offers suggestions for parental involvement to increase learner success.

- Assessment Test. Use the Assessment Test on pages 8 through 11 to determine the skills your students need to practice.

- Language Terms. Provide each student with a copy of the list of language terms on page 12 to keep for reference throughout the year. Also place a copy in the classroom language arts center for reference.

- Center Activities. Use the worksheets as center activities to give students the opportunity to work cooperatively.

- Have fun. The activities use a variety of strategies to maintain student interest. Watch your students' language improve as skills are applied in structured, relevant practice!

Dear Parent,

During this school year, our class will be working with a language program that covers the basics of effective writing and speaking. To increase your child's language skills, we will be completing activity sheets that provide practice to ensure mastery of these important skills.

From time to time, I may send home activity sheets. To best help your child, please consider the following suggestions:

- Provide a quiet place to work.
- Go over the rules, examples, and directions together.
- Encourage your child to do his or her best.
- Check the lesson when it is complete.
- Go over your child's work, and note improvements as well as concerns.

Help your child maintain a positive attitude about language skills. Let your child know that each lesson provides an opportunity to have fun and to learn. If your child expresses anxiety about these skills, help him or her understand what causes the stress. Then talk about ways to deal with it in a positive way.

Above all, enjoy this time you spend with your child. He or she will feel your support, and skills will improve with each activity completed.

Thank you for your help!

Cordially,

Skills Correlation

	1	2	3	4	5	6	7	8
Vocabulary								
Sound Words (Onomatopoeia)	■							
Rhyming Words	■	■						
Synonyms	■	■	■	■	■	■	■	■
Antonyms	■	■	■	■	■	■	■	■
Homonyms	■	■	■	■	■	■	■	■
Multiple Meanings/Homographs	■	■	■	■	■	■	■	■
Prefixes and Suffixes			■	■	■	■	■	■
Base and Root Words			■	■	■	■	■	■
Compound Words			■	■	■	■	■	■
Contractions			■	■	■	■	■	■
Idioms						■	■	■
Connotation/Denotation						■	■	■
Sentences								
Word Order in Sentences	■	■						
Recognizing a Sentence	■	■	■	■	■	■	■	■
Subjects and Predicates	■	■	■	■	■	■	■	■
Types of Sentences	■	■	■	■	■	■	■	■
Compound/Complex Sentences			■	■	■	■	■	■
Sentence Combining			■	■	■	■	■	■
Run-On Sentences				■	■	■	■	■
Independent and Subordinate Clauses							■	■
Compound Subjects and Predicates						■	■	■
Direct and Indirect Objects							■	■
Inverted Word Order						■	■	■
Grammar and Usage								
Common and Proper Nouns	■	■	■	■	■	■	■	■
Singular and Plural Nouns	■	■	■	■	■	■	■	■
Possessive Nouns				■	■	■	■	■
Appositives						■	■	■
Verbs	■	■	■	■	■	■	■	■
Verb Tense	■	■	■	■	■	■	■	■
Regular/Irregular Verbs	■	■	■	■	■	■	■	■
Subject/Verb Agreement		■	■	■	■	■	■	■
Verb Phrases						■	■	■
Transitive and Intransitive Verbs							■	■
Verbals: Gerunds, Participles, and Infinitives							■	■
Active and Passive Voice							■	■
Mood								■
Pronouns	■	■	■	■	■	■	■	■
Antecedents							■	■
Articles	■	■	■					
Adjectives	■	■	■	■	■	■	■	■
Correct Word Usage (e.g. *may/can, sit/set*)	■	■	■	■	■	■	■	■
Adverbs			■	■	■	■	■	■
Prepositions					■	■	■	■
Prepositional Phrases						■	■	■
Conjunctions						■	■	■
Interjections						■	■	■
Double Negatives								■
Capitalization and Punctuation								
Capitalization: First Word in Sentence	■	■	■	■	■	■	■	
Capitalization: Proper Nouns	■	■	■	■	■	■	■	■
Capitalization: in Letters		■	■	■	■	■	■	■

	1	2	3	4	5	6	7	8
Capitalization and Punctuation (cont'd)								
Capitalization: Abbreviations		■	■	■	■	■	■	■
Capitalization: Titles		■	■	■	■	■	■	■
Capitalization: Proper Adjectives						■	■	■
End Punctuation	■	■	■	■	■	■	■	■
Commas		■	■	■	■	■	■	■
Apostrophes in Contractions		■	■	■	■	■	■	■
Apostrophes in Possessives			■	■	■	■	■	■
Quotation Marks			■	■	■	■	■	■
Colons/Semicolons						■	■	■
Hyphens						■	■	■
Composition								
Expanding Sentences						■	■	■	■
Writing a Paragraph		■	■	■	■	■	■	■
Paragraphs: Topic Sentence (main idea)		■	■	■	■	■	■	■
Paragraphs: Supporting Details		■	■	■	■	■	■	■
Order In Paragraphs		■	■	■	■	■	■	
Writing Process:								
Establishing Purpose		■	■			■	■	■
Audience					■	■	■	■
Topic		■	■	■	■	■	■	
Outlining			■			■	■	■
Clustering/Brainstorming					■			■
Notetaking						■	■	
Revising/Proofreading					■	■	■	■
Types of Writing:								
Letter	■	■	■			■		
"How-to" Paragraph			■					
Invitation			■					
Telephone Message			■					
Conversation				■				
Narrative Paragraph				■				
Comparing and Contrasting					■			
Descriptive Paragraph					■			
Report						■		
Interview							■	
Persuasive Composition								■
Readiness/Study Skills								
Grouping	■							
Letters of Alphabet	■							
Listening	■	■						
Making Comparisons	■	■						
Organizing Information	■	■	■					
Following Directions	■	■	■	■	■			
Alphabetical Order	■	■	■	■	■	■	■	■
Using a Dictionary:								
Definitions		■	■	■	■	■	■	■
Guide Words/Entry Words		■	■	■	■	■	■	■
Syllables			■	■	■	■	■	■
Multiple Meanings						■	■	■
Word Origins						■	■	■
Parts of a Book						■	■	■
Using the Library						■	■	■
Using Encyclopedias				■	■	■	■	■
Using Reference Books						■	■	■
Using the *Readers' Guide*							■	■
Choosing Appropriate Sources						■	■	■

Name _____   Date _____

Assessment Test

A. Write **S** before each pair of synonyms, **A** before each pair of antonyms, and **H** before each pair of homonyms.

1. _____ aloud, allowed

2. _____ tiny, miniature

3. _____ argumentative, agreeable

4. _____ massive, giant

B. Write the homograph for the pair of meanings.

1. a. to move slowly   **b.** a unit of measurement _____

C. Write **P** before each word with a prefix, **S** before each word with a suffix, and **C** before each compound word.

1. _____ wishful

2. _____ overblown

3. _____ unruly

4. _____ misinform

D. Write the words that make up each contraction.

1. they've _____ _____   **2.** we'll _____ _____

E. Underline the word in parentheses that has the more positive connotation.

The (generous, pushy) baker insisted we try the hot cookies.

F. Circle the letter of the idiom that means <u>depressed</u>.

1. a. down in the dumps   **b.** in the doghouse

G. Write **D** before the declarative sentence, **IM** before the imperative sentence, **E** before the exclamatory sentence, and **IN** before the interrogative sentence. Then underline the simple subject, and circle the simple predicate in each sentence.

1. _____ Look out for that hole!

2. _____ Please hand me the towel.

3. _____ Why are you still here?

4. _____ I usually leave at noon.

H. Write **CS** before the sentence that has a compound subject and **CP** before the sentence that has a compound predicate.

1. _____ Peaches and strawberries are great in pies.

2. _____ We watched and cheered our team.

I. Write **CS** before the compound sentence, **RO** before the run-on sentence, and **I** before the sentence that is in inverted order.

1. _____ You have a toothache, you should go to the dentist.

2. _____ I wanted chocolate, but they only had vanilla.

3. _____ Up the tree scampered the squirrel.

J. Put brackets around the subordinate clause, and underline the independent clause in this complex sentence. Then write **DO** above the direct object.

The doctor handed Jesse the prescription that he needed.

Name _____   Date _____

K. Underline the common nouns, and circle the proper nouns in the sentence.

Ms. Chang rounded up the group and began the tour of the Jefferson Memorial.

L. Circle the appositive in the sentence. Underline the noun it identifies or explains.

My favorite uncle, Tom Fiske, was recently elected mayor of Greenville.

M. Write past, present, or future to show the tense of each underlined verb.

1. _____ Kathy painted one wall in her kitchen pale blue.

2. _____ Peter will call tomorrow morning at eight o'clock.

3. _____ Each morning before breakfast, Juan walks two miles.

4. _____ I will go to the library today.

N. Circle the correct verbs in each sentence.

1. There (is, are) only six weeks left before we (go, went) on vacation.

2. Steve (set, sat) down and (lay, laid) the sleeping kitten in his lap.

3. To (teach, learn) how to ski, you should (take, took) lessons.

4. (Sit, Set) the plate beside the sink where the glasses are (sitting, setting).

O. Circle the number of the sentence that is in the active voice.

1. The packages were sent two weeks ago.

2. Phillip leaped to his feet to disagree with the speaker.

P. Write SP before the sentence that has a subject pronoun, OP before the sentence that has an object pronoun, PP before the sentence that has a possessive pronoun, and IP before the sentence that has an indefinite pronoun. Circle the pronoun in each sentence.

1. _____ Nobody understands what happened.

2. _____ Ellen played the first song for him.

3. _____ The horse raised its head to look at the dog.

4. _____ He sent the memo to four people.

Q. Underline the pronoun. Circle its antecedent.

Janet and Jason met to discuss the response to their request.

R. Write adjective or adverb to describe the underlined word.

1. _____ These days are the best of the summer.

2. _____ Charlotte tiptoed quietly past the open door.

3. _____ That was the most difficult skating move I've ever seen.

4. _____ I really like Canadian bacon on my pizza.

5. _____ The dachshund is a tiny breed of dog.

6. _____ That heavy tree will be extremely hard to move.

S. Underline each prepositional phrase twice. Circle each preposition. Underline the conjunction once.

I don't have the time or the patience to talk about the complaints of those people.

Name _____ Date _____

T. Rewrite the letter. Add capital letters and punctuation where needed.

591 w franklin place
bent tree tx 78709
jan 27 19____

dear ms coleman

    please know that I called you at exactly 915 but nobody answered the phone____ i hope that youll allow me another opportunity to tell you about my work____ i have exciting news____ i won the national photo contest and my picture will be in the next issue of parks of the world____

    i look forward to speaking with you____ please call anytime this week between 1000 and 230____ ill be in one of these places my home my office or my car you have all three numbers____

sincerely
eric flannery

_____

_____

_____

_____

_____

_____

_____

_____

_____

_____

_____

_____

_____

U. Number the sentences in order, with the topic sentence first.

1. _____ Then they walk to find water, and they drink their fill.

2. _____ An elephant herd walks and eats most of the day.

3. _____ The herd wakes early to graze before it gets too hot.

4. _____ Finally, they lie down and sleep.

V. Write brainstorming, outlining, or persuading to describe each of the following.

1. organizing your thoughts before you write _____

2. convincing others to accept a personal opinion _____

3. bringing to mind as many ideas as possible _____

Name _____ Date _____

W. Rewrite the sentence below. Correct the errors in the sentence by following the proofreader's marks.

As the movie began crowd the grew silent and and consentraited on the actshun.

_____

X. Use the dictionary entry to answer the questions.

honor (än′ ər) *n.* **1.** esteem; respect. **2.** recognition [Old French *honor*]

n.	noun
pron.	pronoun
v.	verb
adj.	adjective
adv.	adverb
prep.	preposition

1. What part of speech is the word honor? _____

2. Would honest come before or after honor? _____

3. Which language is in the history of the word honor? _____

4. Write honor separated into syllables. _____

Y. Write the letter of the reference source in the blank before its description.

_____ 1. used to find synonyms and antonyms   **a.** dictionary

_____ 2. lists articles in magazines by author and subject   **b.** card catalog

_____ 3. used to find definitions, pronunciations, and origins of words   **c.** encyclopedia

_____ 4. presents information about geographical locations   **d.** atlas

_____ 5. contains specific yearly information on a variety of topics   **e.** *Readers' Guide*

_____ 6. a source of articles about many different people and things   **f.** almanac

_____ 7. contains information cards on every book in the library   **g.** thesaurus

Z. Use the catalog card below to answer the questions.

759
HES   **Heslewood, Juliet**

      The history of Western painting: a young person's guide.

      Austin, Texas: Raintree/Steck-Vaughn, © 1996.

      64 p. : col. illus.

      Includes bibliographical references and index.

1. What is the title of the book? _____

2. Who is the author? _____

3. Is the book illustrated? _____

4. What is the book's call number? _____

5. When was the book published? _____

6. Who is the publisher? _____

7. How many pages does the book have? _____

Language Terms

abstract noun names an idea, quality, action, or feeling

active voice a sentence in which the subject acts

adjective modifies a noun

adverb modifies a verb, an adjective, or another adverb

antecedent the word to which a pronoun refers

antonym has the opposite meaning of another word

apostrophe a mark used to show where a letter or letters have been left out of a contraction

appositive a noun or phrase that identifies or explains the noun it follows

clause a group of words that contains a subject and a predicate

collective noun names a group of persons or things

common noun names any one of a class of objects

complete predicate the part of a sentence that includes all the words that state action or condition of the subject

complete subject the part of a sentence that includes all the words that tell who or what the sentence is about

complex sentence contains one independent clause and one or more subordinate clauses

compound predicate two or more simple predicates

compound sentence two or more independent clauses

compound subject two or more simple subjects

compound word a word made up of two or more words

concrete noun names things you can see and touch

conjunction a word used to join words or groups of words

connotation suggests something positive or negative

contraction a word formed by joining two other words

declarative sentence a sentence that makes a statement

demonstrative adjective points out a specific person or thing

demonstrative pronoun points out a specific person or thing

denotation the exact meaning of a word

descriptive adjective tells what kind, which one, or how many

direct object who or what receives the action of the verb

exclamatory sentence expresses strong emotion

gerund a verb form ending in -ing used as a noun

helping verb used to help the main verb of the sentence

homograph has the same spelling as another word, but a different meaning and sometimes a different pronunciation

homonym sounds like another word, but has a different meaning and is spelled differently

idiom an expression that has a meaning different from the usual meanings of the individual words within it

imperative mood expresses a command or a request

imperative sentence expresses a command or a request

indefinite pronoun does not refer to a specific person or thing

independent clause a clause that can stand alone as a sentence because it expresses a complete thought

indicative mood states a fact or asks a question

indirect object tells to whom or for whom an action is done

infinitive the base form of the verb, usually preceded by to

interrogative sentence a sentence that asks a question

intransitive verb does not need an object

inverted order the order of a sentence when all or part of the predicate comes before the subject

limiting adjective the articles a, an, and the

mood verb form that shows the manner of doing or being

natural order the order of a sentence when the subject comes before all or part of the predicate

noun a word that names a person, place, thing, or quality

object of the preposition noun or pronoun in the prepositional phrase

object pronoun used after an action verb or preposition

participle a present or past tense verb used as an adjective

passive voice a sentence in which the subject receives the action

possessive noun shows possession of the noun that follows

possessive pronoun used to show ownership

predicate tells what the subject does or what happens to the subject

prefix a syllable added to the beginning of a base word that changes the meaning of the word

preposition a word that shows the relationship of a noun or a pronoun to another word in the sentence

prepositional phrase a group of words that begins with a preposition and ends with a noun or pronoun

pronoun a word that takes the place of a noun

proper adjective adjective formed from a proper noun

proper noun a noun that names a particular person, place, or thing and is capitalized

relative pronoun a pronoun that can introduce a subordinate clause

run-on sentence two or more independent clauses that are run together without correct punctuation

sentence expresses a complete thought

simple predicate the verb in the complete predicate

simple sentence contains only one independent clause

simple subject the main word in the complete subject

subject tells who or what the sentence is about

subject pronoun a pronoun used in the subject of a sentence and after a linking verb

subjunctive mood can indicate a wish or a contrary-to-fact condition

subordinate clause has a subject and predicate but is not a sentence because it does not express a complete thought

suffix a syllable added to the end of a base word that changes the meaning of the word

synonym a word that has the same or nearly the same meaning as one or more other words

transitive verb has a direct object

verb a word that expresses action, being, or state of being

verb phrase a main verb and one or more helping verbs

verb tense tells the time of the action or being

voice relation of a subject to the action expressed by the verb

Unit 2 Test

Choose the correct sentence type.

1. When will you be back?

   A ○ declarative   **C** ○ imperative

   B ○ interrogative   **D** ○ exclamatory

2. What a wonderful surprise!

   A ○ declarative   **C** ○ imperative

   B ○ interrogative   **D** ○ exclamatory

3. Please leave me alone.

   A ○ declarative   **C** ○ imperative

   B ○ interrogative   **D** ○ exclamatory

4. I wish this rain would stop.

   A ○ declarative   **C** ○ imperative

   B ○ interrogative   **D** ○ exclamatory

Choose the sentence in which the complete subject is underlined.

5. **A** ○ The agency designed a beautiful brochure.

   B ○ James and Mary Ellen are twins.

   C ○ Our cars are the same make and model.

   D ○ The end of the movie came all too soon.

Choose the sentence in which the complete predicate is underlined.

6. **A** ○ We spent the day skiing and skating.

   B ○ Please give me your hand.

   C ○ Go ask Erika for the key.

   D ○ First, deliver the letter.

Choose the sentence in which the simple subject is underlined.

7. **A** ○ Those are my brother's records.

   B ○ Your turn is next.

   C ○ There are many varieties of fish.

   D ○ Our house is made of brick.

Choose the sentence in which the simple predicate is underlined.

8. **A** ○ Would you like to go with us?

   B ○ I am not going to the party.

   C ○ Mr. Wong owns a shoe store.

   D ○ When did Trish say good-bye?

Choose the sentence in which the compound subject is underlined.

9. **A** ○ Paul asked his friend to leave.

   B ○ Lily and Dana like to compete.

   C ○ The dog growled and barked.

   D ○ Oatmeal and fruit make a good breakfast.

Choose the sentence in which the compound predicate is underlined.

10. **A** ○ Charles cheered and clapped.

   B ○ They planted and watered the seeds.

   C ○ Sally and Dave agreed to the sale.

   D ○ Why did he grumble and moan?

Choose whether the underlined word is (A) an indirect object, (B) a direct object, or (C) neither.

11. We swam for hours each day at camp.   **A** ○   **B** ○   **C** ○

12. Would you please give me your new phone number?   **A** ○   **B** ○   **C** ○

13. I made my sister a swing from some rope and a board.   **A** ○   **B** ○   **C** ○

14. Last summer I taught children sign language.   **A** ○   **B** ○   **C** ○

15. Did Diane write you a letter while she was away?   **A** ○   **B** ○   **C** ○

Choose (A) if the underlined group of words is an adjective clause or (B) if it is an adverb clause.

16. Although I like to fish, I don't care for baiting the hook.   **A** ○   **B** ○

17. The eagle that soared over our heads was very majestic.   **A** ○   **B** ○

18. We saw several deer after we got far enough into the woods.   **A** ○   **B** ○

19. Dimitri will take our picture when he arrives.   **A** ○   **B** ○

20. She started back home because it was getting late.   **A** ○   **B** ○

21. We left before the rain began.   **A** ○   **B** ○

22. We studied all of the paintings that were in the exhibit.   **A** ○   **B** ○

Choose (A) if the group of words is a compound sentence, (B) if it is a complex sentence, or (C) if it is a sentence in inverted order.

23. Under the porch ran the dog.   **A** ○   **B** ○   **C** ○

24. Did you see the geese this morning?   **A** ○   **B** ○   **C** ○

25. I would like to meet Kate, but she left for Canada today.   **A** ○   **B** ○   **C** ○

26. Tom is picking up litter in the alley, and he will be finished soon.   **A** ○   **B** ○   **C** ○

27. Over the steep hill came the speeding truck.   **A** ○   **B** ○   **C** ○

28. I can't wait; summer vacation starts in May.   **A** ○   **B** ○   **C** ○

29. Tim will come to get you when he is ready.   **A** ○   **B** ○   **C** ○

30. They are the ones who started this project.   **A** ○   **B** ○   **C** ○

Choose the sentence that is a run-on sentence.

31. **A** ○ Have you ever seen the Leaning Tower of Pisa in Pisa, Italy?

     B ○ It's considered one of seven wonders of the world, it leans very far to one side.

     C ○ After three of its stories were built, the ground beneath the tower began to sink.

     D ○ Many say that Galileo conducted his experiments from this tower; others disagree.

32. **A** ○ The city council will vote today on building a new office, we hope they don't.

     B ○ Last year they decided they needed more space, but the public didn't approve.

     C ○ It almost seems as if they don't care what we think, doesn't it?

     D ○ The solution may be to vote them all out of office during the next election.

33. **A** ○ James and Sabrina decided to have a dinner party.

     B ○ They made a list of everything they would need.

     C ○ They went to the grocery store, they bought everything on the list.

     D ○ Everyone who went had a great time.

Common and Proper Nouns

> - There are two main classes of nouns: **common** and **proper nouns.**
> - A **common noun** names any one of a class of objects.
>   EXAMPLES: woman, city, tree
> - A **proper noun** names a particular person, place, or thing. It begins with a capital letter.
>   EXAMPLES: Ms. Patel, Chicago, Empire State Building

A. Underline each noun. Then write C or P above it to show whether it is a common or proper noun.

     P   C

1. Maria is my sister.

2. Honolulu is the chief city and capital of Hawaii.

3. Rainbow Natural Bridge is hidden away in the wild mountainous part of southern Utah.

4. The Declaration of Independence is often called the birth certificate of the United States.

5. Abraham Lincoln, Edgar Allan Poe, and Frederic Chopin were born in the same year.

B. Write a proper noun suggested by each common noun.

1. country _____

2. book _____

3. governor _____

4. state _____

5. athlete _____

6. school _____

7. actor _____

8. day _____

9. car _____

10. lake _____

11. singer _____

12. holiday _____

13. newspaper _____

14. river _____

C. Write a sentence using each proper noun and the common noun for its class.

1. Mexico   Mexico is another country in North America. _____

2. December _____

3. Alaska _____

4. Thanksgiving Day _____

5. Bill Clinton _____

6. Tuesday _____

Concrete, Abstract, and Collective Nouns

> - A **concrete noun** names things you can see and touch.
>   EXAMPLES: apple, dog, fork, book, computer
> - An **abstract noun** names an idea, quality, action, or feeling.
>   EXAMPLES: bravery, wickedness, goodness
> - A **collective noun** names a group of persons or things.
>   EXAMPLES: crowd, congress, public, United States

- **Classify each common noun as concrete, collective, or abstract.**

1. humor _____
2. kindness _____
3. army _____
4. danger _____
5. committee _____
6. towel _____
7. jury _____
8. audience _____
9. bird _____
10. orchestra _____
11. fear _____
12. family _____
13. happiness _____
14. truck _____
15. team _____
16. honesty _____
17. bracelet _____
18. society _____
19. album _____
20. courage _____
21. faculty _____

22. club _____
23. photograph _____
24. poverty _____
25. class _____
26. swarm _____
27. table _____
28. goodness _____
29. flock _____
30. radio _____
31. mob _____
32. patience _____
33. herd _____
34. banana _____
35. staff _____
36. mercy _____
37. calculator _____
38. coyote _____
39. generosity _____
40. scissors _____
41. sorrow _____
42. independence _____

Singular and Plural Nouns

Noun	Plural Form	Examples
■ The following chart shows how to change **singular nouns** into **plural nouns.**		
Most nouns	Add -s	ship, ships nose, noses
Nouns ending in a consonant and -y	Change the -y to -i, and add -es	sky, skies navy, navies
Nouns ending in -o	Add -s or -es	hero, heroes piano, pianos
Most nouns ending in -f or -fe	Change the -f or -fe to -ves	half, halves
Most nouns ending in -ch, -sh, -s, or -x	Add -es	bench, benches bush, bushes tax, taxes
Many two-word or three-word compound nouns	Add -s to the principle word	son-in-law, sons-in-law
Nouns with the same form in the singular and plural	No change	sheep
Nouns with no singular form	No change	scissors
Nouns with irregular plurals	Change the entire word	foot, feet child, children
Figures, symbols, signs, letters, and words considered as words	Add an apostrophe and -s	m, m's 5, 5's and, and's

A. Write the plural for each singular noun.

1. county _____

2. pony _____

3. tomato _____

4. banjo _____

5. match _____

6. window _____

7. century _____

8. trench _____

9. bookcase _____

10. video _____

11. radio _____

12. farm _____

13. fly _____

14. hero _____

15. dress _____

16. boot _____

17. desk _____

18. daisy _____

Name _____   Date _____

B. Write the singular form of each word below.

1. mouthfuls _____   9. wolves _____

2. proofs _____   10. roofs _____

3. 6's _____   11. gentlemen _____

4. calves _____   12. editors-in-chief _____

5. knives _____   13. +'s _____

6. Joneses _____   14. cupfuls _____

7. children _____   15. trout _____

8. geese _____   16. mice _____

C. Fill each blank with the plural form of the word in parentheses. You may use a dictionary to check spellings.

1. (box) Please store these _____ in the garage.

2. (city) Can you name the four largest _____ in your state?

3. (deer) The photographers brought back photos of three _____.

4. (flash) The vivid _____ of lightning frightened everyone.

5. (coach) That football team employs five _____.

6. (church) Our small town has several beautiful _____.

7. (potato) Hot _____ were used as hand warmers in colonial days.

8. (e) How many _____ are in the word <u>Tennessee</u>?

9. (O'Keefe) The _____ are having a recital tonight.

10. (fish) Where did you catch those _____?

11. (scarf) Dale gave me three _____.

12. (n) Cynthia, don't make your _____ look like <u>u</u>'s.

13. (radio) Kirk listens to two _____ so he can hear all the news.

14. (ox) The _____ wore a yoke around their necks.

15. (pilot) Those _____ flew four round trips a day.

16. (90) The teacher gave three _____ on the math test.

17. (woman) A dozen _____ attended the conference.

18. (i) Be sure to always dot your _____.

Possessive Nouns

> - A **possessive noun** shows possession of the noun that follows.
>   EXAMPLES: Gerry's football, Donna's gloves
> - Form the possessive of most singular nouns by adding an apostrophe
>   (') and -s.
>   EXAMPLES: José's pillow, Sandy's eyes
> - Form the possessive of most plural nouns ending in -s by adding only
>   an apostrophe.
>   EXAMPLES: birds' nest, lions' den
> - Form the possessive of plural nouns that do not end in -s by adding
>   apostrophe and -s.
>   EXAMPLES: men's wear

- **Underline the possessive nouns in each sentence.**

1. Steve's glasses are on my desk.

2. Mary is wearing her mother's gold bracelet.

3. My friends' club will meet at our house Monday night.

4. The woman's first statement caused us to change our minds.

5. We have formed a collector's club.

6. Rosa's brother found the child's lost puppy.

7. The Warrens' store was damaged by the recent storm.

8. What are the vice-president's duties?

9. When does the new mayor's term of office begin?

10. Lee, Tony's notebook is on your desk.

11. We went to the women's department.

12. The family's income was reduced.

13. Our day's work is done.

14. The lifeguards' heroism was rewarded.

15. Our team's defeat did not discourage us.

16. Has Joanna opened a children's store?

17. Juan's cooking is improving.

18. We borrowed Jim's hammer.

19. May I see Calvin's picture?

20. I'll meet you at the Lees'.

21. Lucy visited Mark's college.

22. Frank's telephone call was about Jean's accident.

23. Mr. Clark stood at his neighbors' gate.

24. Is that the Masons' parking place?

25. The United States' flag has stars and stripes.

Appositives

> ■ An **appositive** is a noun or pronoun that identifies or explains the noun or pronoun it follows.
>   EXAMPLE: My German friend, **Ulrike**, is coming to visit me next month.
> ■ An **appositive phrase** consists of an appositive and its modifiers.
>   EXAMPLE: Peter's school, **the junior high,** is sponsoring a dance.
> ■ Use commas to set off an appositive or an appositive phrase that is not essential to the meaning of the sentence.
>   EXAMPLE: Rico's nephew, **a twelve-year-old,** delivers newspapers.
> ■ Do not use commas if the appositive is essential to the meaning of the sentence.
>   EXAMPLE: The artist **Picasso** is my favorite.

■ **Underline each appositive word or phrase, and circle the noun it identifies.**

1. (Jan Matzeliger), the inventor of the first shoemaking machine, was born in South America.

2. Niagara Falls, the waterfalls in New York, is not the tallest in the country.

3. Harvard, the oldest university in the United States, is in Massachusetts.

4. My brother Jim lives in Connecticut.

5. Diane Feinstein, a mayor of San Francisco, was San Francisco's first woman mayor.

6. The Sears Tower, the tallest building in the world, is in Chicago.

7. Scott's cousin Liz sells antique cars.

8. Leontyne Price, the opera singer, was born in Mississippi.

9. The Pilgrim's ship the *Mayflower* had a stormy voyage.

10. Tom's dog Jasmine likes to swim.

11. Dr. Miller, our family physician, is attending a convention with her husband.

12. The swimmer Mark Spitz won seven gold medals in one Olympics.

13. Fort Worth, a city in Texas, is almost midway between the Atlantic and the Pacific.

14. Aunt Lee, my father's sister, is coming to visit.

15. Mr. Diddon, coach of the hockey team, has never had a losing season.

16. Monticello, Jefferson's home, is an example of colonial architecture.

17. The inventor Thomas Edison is responsible for many electrical breakthroughs.

18. Athens, the leading city of ancient Greece, was a center of culture.

19. The Aztec king Montezuma was captured by Cortez.

20. The boll weevil, a small beetle, causes great damage to cotton.

21. The Hoover Dam, a dam in the Colorado River, took five years to build.

22. Antares, a star many times larger than the sun, is the red star in Scorpio.

23. The composer Mozart lived a short but productive life.

24. That is a copperhead, one of the four poisonous snakes found in the United States.

25. Mt. McKinley, a rugged mountain, is the tallest mountain in North America.

Name _____ Date _____

Verbs

- A **verb** is a word that expresses action, being, or state of being.
  EXAMPLES: Leo **traveled** to Europe. Maura **is** an accountant.
- A verb has four principal parts: **present, present participle, past,** and **past participle.**
- For regular verbs, form the present participle by adding -ing to the present. Use a form of the helping verb be with the present participle.
- Form the past and past participle by adding -ed to the present. Use a form of the helping verb have with the past participle.
  EXAMPLES:

Present	Present Participle	Past	Past Participle
listen	(is) listening	listened	(have, had, has) listened
help	(is) helping	helped	(have, had, has) helped
change	(is) changing	changed	(have, had, has) changed

- Irregular verbs form their past and past participle in other ways. A dictionary shows the principal parts of these verbs.

- **Write the present participle, past, and past participle for each verb.**

PRESENT	PRESENT PARTICIPLE	PAST	PAST PARTICIPLE
1. scatter	(is) scattering	scattered	(have, had, has) scattered
2. express			
3. paint			
4. call			
5. cook			
6. observe			
7. look			
8. walk			
9. ramble			
10. shout			
11. notice			
12. order			
13. gaze			
14. borrow			
15. start			
16. work			

Verb Phrases

- A **verb phrase** consists of a main verb and one or more **helping verbs.** A helping verb is also called an **auxiliary verb.** In a verb phrase, the helping verb or verbs precede the main verb.
  EXAMPLE: Liz **has been** reading a mystery.
- The helping verbs are
  am, are, is, was, were, be, being, been
  has, have, had
  do, does, did
  can, could, must, may, might
  shall, should, will, would

A. Underline each verb or verb phrase, and circle each helping verb in the sentences below.

1. Most people have heard the story of Jonathan Chapman.

2. He was born in 1775 and has become an American legend.

3. You may have heard of him as the barefooted, lovable Johnny Appleseed.

4. As Jonathan Chapman, he had grown up in the woods near Boston, Massachusetts.

5. He had learned about fruit trees in the orchards near his family's farm.

6. He was always interested in the stories he had heard about the Great West.

7. As a young man, he had declared, "I will go west to Pennsylvania and plant my own orchard."

8. Jonathan had done just that, but in a few years, the wilderness had moved farther west.

9. "What should I do now?" Jonathan asked himself.

10. "I will plant other apple orchards!" was his answer.

11. Jonathan could not remain content.

12. Soon he was traveling with the other settlers as the frontier pushed farther and farther west.

13. People called him Johnny Appleseed, that odd man who did not have a home.

14. He would sleep out in the open with his beloved trees.

B. Use each verb phrase in a sentence.

1. should learn _____

2. will occur _____

3. may find _____

4. have tried _____

5. can make _____

6. will go _____

Verb Tenses

- The **tense** of a verb tells the time of the action or being. There are six main tenses: **present, past, future, present perfect, past perfect,** and **future prefect.**
- Present tense tells about what is happening now.
  EXAMPLES: Emily **sings.** The kittens **are playing.**
- Past tense tells about something that happened in the past.
  EXAMPLES: Emily **sang** in the play. The kittens **were playing** on the porch.
- Future tense tells about something that will happen in the future.
  EXAMPLES: Emily **will sing** in the play. The kittens **will play** on the porch.
- Present perfect tense tells about something that occurred at an indefinite time in the past.
  EXAMPLE: Emily **has sung** the song.
  It is also used to tell about something that began in the past and continues in the present.
  EXAMPLE: The kittens **have been playing** on the porch.
- Past perfect tense tells about something completed at some past time before something else.
  EXAMPLES: Emily **had sung** before you arrived. The kittens **had been playing** on the porch until Tom came home.
- Future perfect tense tells about something that will be completed before some definite future time.
  EXAMPLES: Emily **will have finished** singing by eight o'clock.

- **Underline each verb or verb phrase. Write <u>present</u>, <u>past</u>, <u>future</u>, <u>present perfect</u>, <u>past perfect</u>, or <u>future perfect</u>.**

1. I <u>brought</u> these vegetables. _____past_____

2. Yes, I know her. _____

3. They will close the office tomorrow. _____

4. The work will continue for several days. _____

5. His friend has donated the painting to the museum. _____

6. Alex had told us many stories about his travels. _____

7. Jesse Owens was a famous track star. _____

8. She sings well. _____

9. Mark will have paid for the meal. _____

10. I will have been in St. Louis for a week. _____

11. The neighborhood children had been playing baseball. _____

12. I have anchored the boat. _____

Name _____   Date _____

Using Irregular Verbs

A. Write the principal parts of each verb. You may use a dictionary.

PRESENT	PRESENT PARTICIPLE	PAST	PAST PARTICIPLE
1. do	is doing	did	has done
2. come	_____	_____	_____
3. eat	_____	_____	_____
4. go	_____	_____	_____
5. see	_____	_____	_____
6. take	_____	_____	_____

B. Fill in the blank with the correct form of the verb in parentheses.

1. (see) I had never _____ the waterfall before.

2. (see) Have you ever _____ a helicopter?

3. (take) Laura is _____ the hammer with her.

4. (see) We have just _____ a passenger train going over the bridge.

5. (eat) Haven't you _____ your lunch?

6. (go) You should have _____ with us, Jerry.

7. (go) Jaime is _____ to a committee meeting.

8. (eat) Have you ever _____ a spiced olive?

9. (go) Julian has _____ to play a video game.

10. (take) Carey is _____ the photograph now.

11. (do) Who _____ the landscaping around this building?

12. (do) We have _____ a great deal of outside reading on the topic for discussion.

13. (take) Aren't we _____ the wrong road?

14. (come) People have _____ from every state to see the Carlsbad Caverns.

15. (eat) We had _____ different foods in different areas of the country.

16. (see) Thomas, you should have _____ the last game.

17. (come) Most of our people _____ this way on the way to the park.

18. (do) Matt _____ his best to beat his own record in the broad jump.

Name _____ Date _____

C. Write the principal parts of each verb. You may use a dictionary.

PRESENT	PRESENT PARTICIPLE	PAST	PAST PARTICIPLE
1. begin	_____	_____	_____
2. drink	_____	_____	_____
3. drive	_____	_____	_____
4. give	_____	_____	_____
5. run	_____	_____	_____

D. Fill in the blank with the correct form of the verb in parentheses.

1. (give) My friend _____ this poem to me.

2. (run) The excited children _____ down the street.

3. (begin) Work on the new building had _____ this week.

4. (begin) I _____ this project yesterday.

5. (drink) Haven't you _____ some of this delicious fruit juice?

6. (drive) Steven, have you ever _____ a car?

7. (give) Gwendolyn Brooks has _____ us many interesting poems.

8. (begin) The supervisor of the crew is _____ to explain the work orders.

9. (run) Rachel, have you _____ into Aunt Sarah?

10. (run) The girl _____ to meet her parents.

11. (begin) That problem _____ last year.

12. (give) James has _____ me a painting for my living room.

13. (begin) Look, it is _____ to rain.

14. (run) They _____ hard to get out of the rain.

15. (give) Mrs. Williams has _____ me a job in her store.

16. (give) Donald, who _____ you this watch?

17. (begin) We haven't _____ eating all the bananas.

18. (drink) Have you _____ from this cup?

19. (begin) We _____ raking the leaves this morning.

20. (run) Michelle is _____ in the 2-mile race.

Name _____   Date _____

E. Write the principal parts of each verb. You may use a dictionary.

PRESENT	PRESENT PARTICIPLE	PAST	PAST PARTICIPLE
1. grow	_____	_____	_____
2. know	_____	_____	_____
3. ring	_____	_____	_____
4. sing	_____	_____	_____
5. speak	_____	_____	_____

F. Fill in the blank with the correct form of the verb in parentheses.

1. (sing) Have you ever _____ a solo?

2. (grow) In several minutes, my eyes _____ accustomed to the dark.

3. (know) Bob _____ the answer.

4. (grow) It has _____ very cold during the last hour.

5. (sing) Ricardo is _____ although his throat is sore.

6. (ring) Why hasn't the bell _____?

7. (grow) Lettuce had first _____ in China.

8. (speak) Cynthia _____ to Jonathan yesterday.

9. (ring) The carrier _____ the doorbell.

10. (speak) Has Rafael _____ to you about his promotion?

11. (speak) A police officer is _____ to a group of concerned citizens.

12. (sing) Natalie and her sister _____ on a local TV program last week.

13. (know) We have _____ the members of that family a long time.

14. (ring) The mission bells _____ each morning last week.

15. (throw) Have you _____ away this morning's paper?

16. (grow) Charles, I believe you have _____ a prize-winning rose.

17. (know) We have _____ Roberto's brother for three years.

18. (grow) Because of the rains, the grass is _____ rapidly.

19. (ring) We _____ the doorbell, but no one answered it.

20. (speak) Joan has _____ of you quite often, Jeffrey.

Name _____ Date _____

G. Write the principal parts of each verb. You may use a dictionary.

PRESENT	PRESENT PARTICIPLE	PAST	PAST PARTICIPLE
1. blow	_____	_____	_____
2. break	_____	_____	_____
3. choose	_____	_____	_____
4. draw	_____	_____	_____
5. fly	_____	_____	_____

H. Fill in the blank with the correct form of the verb in parentheses.

1. (draw)   Kim has _____ many cartoons for the daily paper.

2. (blow)   The storm _____ tumbleweeds across the prairie.

3. (fly)   The tiny mockingbird is _____ from its nest.

4. (choose)   We _____ only willing persons for the committee.

5. (choose)   Our club has _____ a motto.

6. (blow)   Has the five o'clock whistle _____?

7. (break)   I accidentally _____ my sister's antique vase.

8. (break)   Her promise had not been _____.

9. (choose)   The coach is _____ the line-up for today's game.

10. (draw)   A famous artist _____ these sketches.

11. (break)   One of the windows in the house had _____ during the storm.

12. (break)   The handle of my hammer _____ while I was using it.

13. (choose)   Has anyone _____ the salad for lunch?

14. (break)   Suzanne _____ this chair yesterday.

15. (freeze)   Those pipes _____ last February.

16. (choose)   Do you think I have _____ wisely?

17. (break)   They _____ our winning streak last week.

18. (draw)   Have you _____ your map, Lee?

19. (break)   Who is _____ these windows?

20. (draw)   Their plans for the new house have been _____.

Name _____ Date _____

I. Write the principal parts of each verb. You may use a dictionary.

PRESENT	PRESENT PARTICIPLE	PAST	PAST PARTICIPLE
1. become	_____	_____	_____
2. fall	_____	_____	_____
3. ride	_____	_____	_____
4. rise	_____	_____	_____
5. steal	_____	_____	_____
6. show	_____	_____	_____
7. sink	_____	_____	_____
8. swim	_____	_____	_____
9. tear	_____	_____	_____
10. wear	_____	_____	_____

J. Fill in the blank with the correct form of the verb in parentheses.

1. (ride)   Have you ever _____ on a tractor?

2. (rise)   The temperature has _____ ten degrees this afternoon.

3. (wear)   We _____ our sweaters because the night air was very cool.

4. (steal)   Look! Carolyn has _____ third base!

5. (ride)   How far are we _____ today?

6. (swim)   Jeanne is _____ around the pool.

7. (tear)   The child _____ his jeans when he fell down.

8. (sink)   When his boat _____, Crusoe was tossed about in the sea.

9. (steal)   Our new car has been _____.

10. (ride)   Have you ever _____ in an airplane?

11. (wear)   This wire has almost been _____ in two.

12. (wear)   I have _____ this coat for several winters.

13. (rise)   The river recently _____ beyond the flood stage.

14. (rise)   Diane has _____ from editor to president of the company.

15. (fall)   All the pears have _____ from the tree.

Mood

> ■ **Mood** is a form of the verb that shows the manner of doing or being. There are three types of moods: **indicative, subjunctive,** and **imperative.**
> ■ **Indicative mood** states a fact or asks a question.
>   EXAMPLES: Ben **came** Friday. How many **went** to the meeting?
> ■ **Subjunctive mood** can indicate a wish or a contrary-to-fact condition. Use <u>were</u> to express the subjunctive.
>   EXAMPLE: I would help you, if I **were** able. (I am not able.)
> ■ **Imperative mood** expresses a command or a request.
>   EXAMPLES: **Ask** no more questions. Let's **start** immediately.

■ **Give the mood of each underlined word.**

1. <u>Come</u> here at once. _____

2. I <u>did</u> not <u>see</u> Carolyn. _____

3. If I <u>were</u> not so tired, I would go to a movie. _____

4. <u>Call</u> for him at once. _____

5. Where <u>has</u> Brittany <u>moved</u>? _____

6. Who <u>invented</u> the sewing machine? _____

7. Juanita <u>came</u> Saturday. _____

8. Paul wishes it <u>were</u> true. _____

9. <u>Come</u> here, Jennifer. _____

10. I wish it <u>were</u> summer. _____

11. <u>Be</u> home early. _____

12. <u>Ring</u> the bell immediately. _____

13. The members of the band <u>sold</u> birthday calendars. _____

14. If I <u>were</u> you, I'd stop that. _____

15. Zachary <u>likes</u> my new sweater. _____

16. My friends <u>painted</u> the entire house. _____

17. If this <u>were</u> a sunny day, I would go with you. _____

18. <u>Tell</u> us where you went. _____

19. He greeted me as though I <u>were</u> a stranger. _____

Name _____   Date _____

Transitive and Intransitive Verbs

- There are two kinds of action verbs: **transitive** and **intransitive**.
- A transitive verb has a direct object.
  EXAMPLE: Columbus **discovered** America.
- An intransitive verb does not need an object to complete its meaning.
  Linking verbs are always intransitive.
  EXAMPLES: The wind **howled**. He **is** afraid.

A. Underline each verb, and classify it as transitive or intransitive.

1. We walked into the new school. _____intransitive_____

2. Ornithology is the study of birds. _____

3. Move those blocks now! _____

4. Everyone listened carefully. _____

5. The workers wore special uniforms. _____

6. We built a barbecue pit in our backyard. _____

7. What is the name of this picture? _____

8. He lives in Germany. _____

9. Who elected the principal of Stuart High? _____

10. Leroy paid the bill. _____

11. We send many good customers to them. _____

12. London is the capital city of Great Britain. _____

13. Frank drew many excellent cartoons. _____

14. We study hard for tests. _____

15. The frightened children cried loudly. _____

16. Lora made this poster. _____

17. Thousands of people ran in the race. _____

18. We learned three new songs. _____

19. The stray dogs barked. _____

20. Please bring me a book about famous Canadian scientists. _____

21. Joseph baked a lemon meringue pie. _____

Name _____   Date _____

B. Underline each verb or verb phrase, and classify it as transitive or intransitive.

1. The President of the United States signed the new law. _____

2. The workers repaired the telephone lines. _____

3. The factory shipped the shoes. _____

4. Wasteful cutting of timber may cause a shortage of lumber. _____

5. Wolf was Rip Van Winkle's sole friend. _____

6. The city of Mobile, Alabama, has a wonderful harbor. _____

7. Explain your meaning, please. _____

8. The wind whistled down the chimney. _____

9. The heavy floods blocked traffic for miles. _____

10. Many leaves have dropped in our yard. _____

11. Inventions change our way of living. _____

12. Birmingham, England, attracts many tourists. _____

13. Dorothea Lange was a famous photographer. _____

14. Julio has a fine collection of coins. _____

15. Who invented the lightning rod? _____

16. We cooked our steaks over an open fire. _____

17. Madame Curie discovered radium. _____

18. Gene traveled through North America and South America. _____

19. Cole Porter composed "Night and Day." _____

20. Amelia Earhart was a famous pilot. _____

21. The tornado destroyed several stores. _____

22. Paul exercises every day. _____

23. We talked for hours. _____

24. Have you ever seen Plymouth Rock? _____

25. Abandoned campfires often cause great forest fires. _____

26. He is studying hard for the exam. _____

27. The United States bought Alaska in 1867. _____

Name _____   Date _____

Active and Passive Voice

- **Voice** refers to the relation of a subject to the action expressed by the verb.
- In the **active voice,** the subject does the action.
  EXAMPLE: The club **made** these decorations.
- In the **passive voice,** the subject is acted upon.
  EXAMPLE: These decorations **were made** by the club.
- Only transitive verbs can be used in the passive voice.

■ Underline each verb. Then write <u>active</u> or <u>passive</u>.

_____passive_____ **1.** The phonograph <u>was invented</u> by Edison.

_____ **2.** Tim hit a home run.

_____ **3.** The bell was rung by the caretaker.

_____ **4.** The football was thrown out of bounds.

_____ **5.** Ricardo has bought some new fishing tackle.

_____ **6.** The decision of the committee was announced yesterday.

_____ **7.** Steve blamed Paul for making him late.

_____ **8.** The first three people were selected for the job openings.

_____ **9.** Carl typed the letter.

_____ **10.** Angela quickly stated the reason for not attending.

_____ **11.** Andrew flopped into the chair.

_____ **12.** Many songs were written by Foster.

_____ **13.** The police officer gave me a ticket.

_____ **14.** Dr. Koneru held a press conference.

_____ **15.** Rosa has bought a new car.

_____ **16.** His heart was broken by the cruelty of his friends.

_____ **17.** Senator Dale shook their hands.

_____ **18.** The boat was carried to the landing.

_____ **19.** The party was given for her birthday.

_____ **20.** Pam wrote the winning essay.

Using *Sit/Set* and *Learn/Teach*

- The verb sit means "to take a resting position."
  - EXAMPLE: Please **sit** in that chair.
- The verb set means "to place."
  - EXAMPLE: **Set** the cups on the saucers.
- The verb learn means "to acquire knowledge."
  - EXAMPLE: I want to **learn** how to tap dance.
- The verb teach means "to give knowledge to" or "to instruct."
  - EXAMPLE: Please **teach** me to tap dance.

Present	Present Participle	Past	Past Participle
sit	sitting	sat	(have) sat
set	setting	set	(have) set
learn	learning	learned	(have) learned
teach	teaching	taught	(have) taught

- **Circle the correct word in parentheses.**

1. Please (sit, set) this table on the patio.

2. My friend is (learning, teaching) us to swim this summer.

3. You should (learn, teach) to eat more slowly.

4. Where do you prefer to (sit, set)?

5. The little dog is always found (sitting, setting) by its owner.

6. Such an experience should (learn, teach) you a lesson.

7. In a theater I always like to (sit, set) near the aisle.

8. I (sat, set) in a reserved seat at the last game.

9. Let me (learn, teach) you a shorter way to do this.

10. Alberto, please (sit, set) down on the step.

11. If you (learn, teach) me how to play tennis, I'll try to (learn, teach) well.

12. With tired sighs, we (sat, set) down on the couch.

13. Andrew, have you (sit, set) out the plants?

14. Jerry, did you (learn, teach) your dog all these tricks?

15. We watched the workers as they (sat, set) stone upon stone.

16. Marcy has (learned, taught) me to water-ski.

17. You can (learn, teach) some animals more easily than others.

18. Mona, do you like to (sit, set) by the window?

19. The first-aid course has (learned, taught) me important procedures.

20. Who (learned, taught) you how to ride a bike?

21. Please (sit, set) these chairs on the rug.

22. Manuel has (sat, set) his work aside.

23. Claire is (learning, teaching) children how to sail in August.

24. All the students are (sitting, setting) quietly.

Pronouns

> - A **pronoun** is a word used in place of a noun.
> - A **personal pronoun** is chosen based on the way it is used in the sentence.
>   A **subject pronoun** is used in the subject of a sentence and after a linking verb.
>   EXAMPLES: **He** is a chemist. The chemist is **he.**
>   An **object pronoun** is used after an action verb or a preposition.
>   EXAMPLES: Jan gave **me** the gift. Jan gave the gift to **me.**
>   A **possessive pronoun** is used to show ownership of something.
>   EXAMPLES: The new car is **ours.** That is **our** car.

- **Underline each pronoun.**

1. Brian, do you have my ticket to the play?

2. Just between you and me, I want to go with them.

3. Carol, will you help me carry our trunk?

4. May I go with you?

5. I saw him standing in line to go to a movie.

6. Just be sure to find Carol and me.

7. We will be ready when they come for us.

8. She sent this box of frozen steaks to Andrea and me.

9. She asked you and me to be on her bowling team.

10. We saw them go into the building on the corner.

11. Last week we sent flowers to our sick friend.

12. He must choose their dinner.

13. She is my English instructor.

14. They have never invited us to go with them.

15. The first-place winner is she.

16. Can he compete against you?

17. She made the dinner for us.

18. Liz and I are going on vacation in June.

19. Where is your umbrella?

20. Sharon gave me a book to read.

21. Do you know where our cottage is?

22. If I lend you my car, will you take care of it?

23. I gave him my word that we would visit her.

24. When they saw us fishing, Bob and Diane changed their clothes.

25. Your toes are peeking through your socks.

26. Marie showed us how to fasten her bike to our car.

Using *Its* and *It's*

> ■ It's is a contraction for "it is."   EXAMPLE: **It's** a beautiful day.
> ■ <u>Its</u> is a personal pronoun.   EXAMPLE: The dog hurt **its** leg.

A. Underline the correct word in each sentence.

1. Our town is proud of (its, it's) elected officials.

2. (Its, It's) time for the curtain to rise.

3. Tell me when (its, it's) time for that television program.

4. (Its, It's) a mile from our house to the grocery store.

5. I think (its, it's) too cold to walk.

6. (Its, It's) almost time for the show to start.

7. (Its, It's) noon already.

8. (Its, It's) time to give the puppy (its, it's) bath.

9. The cat is playing with (its, it's) toy.

10. (Its, It's) time for us to start home.

11. It looks like (its, it's) going to rain.

12. This dog has lost (its, it's) collar.

13. I think that bird has hurt (its, it's) wing.

14. I do believe (its, it's) getting colder.

15. The dog is looking for (its, it's) owner.

16. (Its, It's) a long and very interesting story.

17. Do you know (its, it's) color was green?

18. The pony shook (its, it's) head and ran to the stable.

19. Do you think (its, it's) too late to call?

20. The bear cub imitated (its, it's) mother.

B. Write three sentences of your own in which you use <u>its</u>.

1. _____

2. _____

3. _____

C. Write three sentences of your own in which you use <u>it's</u>.

1. _____

2. _____

3. _____

Demonstrative and Indefinite Pronouns

- A **demonstrative pronoun** is used to point out a specific person or thing.
- This and that are used in place of singular nouns. This refers to a person or thing nearby, and that refers to a person or thing farther away.
    - EXAMPLES: **This** is mine. **That** is the right one.
- These and those are used in place of plural nouns. These points to persons or things nearby, and those points to persons or things farther away.
    - EXAMPLES: **These** are the best ones. **Those** don't look ripe.

A. Underline each demonstrative pronoun.

1. Those are the books I lost.

2. That is where Anne lives.

3. I'm not sure these are my scissors.

4. This is my pen; that is Pam's book.

5. I think those are interesting books.

6. Is that your first mistake?

7. This is Gretchen's timecard.

8. Give these to your friend.

9. These are Stephanie's shoes.

10. Please don't mention this.

11. I think those are just rumors.

12. Will this be our last chance?

13. Dave, those are your messages.

14. These are large peaches.

15. Sorry, that was my last piece.

16. Who told you that?

- An **indefinite pronoun** does not refer to a specific person or thing.
    - EXAMPLE: **Many** are called, but **few** are chosen.
- The indefinite pronouns anybody, anyone, anything, each, everyone, everybody, everything, nobody, no one, nothing, one, somebody, someone, and something are singular. They take singular verbs.
    - EXAMPLE: **Everyone is** ready.
- The indefinite pronouns both, few, many, several, and some are plural. They take plural verbs.
    - EXAMPLE: **Several are** ready.

B. Underline each indefinite pronoun.

1. Both worked hard.

2. Let each help decorate.

3. Several have called about the job.

4. Unfortunately, some never learn.

5. Everyone was delighted at our party.

6. I think someone forgot this sweater.

7. Some asked for pens.

8. He thinks that each is right.

9. Has anyone seen my wallet?

10. Will someone wash the dishes?

11. Both of the singers are here.

12. One is absent.

13. Each must carry a bag.

14. Some always succeed.

15. Did someone leave this lunch?

16. Everybody is to be here early.

Antecedents

- An **antecedent** is the word to which a pronoun refers.
  EXAMPLE: **Stars** are lovely when **they** shine.
- A pronoun must agree with its antecedent in **gender (masculine,**
  feminine, or **neuter)** and **number (singular** or **plural).**
  EXAMPLES: **Susan** helped **her** friend. The **people** went in **their** cars.
- If the antecedent is an indefinite pronoun, it is correct to use a
  masculine pronoun. However, it is now common to use both a
  masculine and feminine pronoun.
  EXAMPLES: **Someone** lost **his** dog. **Someone** lost **his or her** dog.

- **Underline the correct pronoun, and circle its antecedent.**

1. (Everyone) should work hard at (their, <u>his or her</u>) job.

2. Each of the children willingly did (his or her, their) share of the camp duties.

3. Sophia gave me (her, their) coat to wear.

4. I took (my, our) friend to the ceremony.

5. All members were asked to bring (his or her, their) contributions today.

6. The women have had (her, their) vacation.

7. Someone has left (her or his, their) automobile across the driveway.

8. If each does (his or her, their) best, our chorus will win.

9. Would you tell Joanne that (her, his) soup is ready?

10. Every woman did (her, their) best to make the program a success.

11. Never judge anyone entirely by (his or her, their) looks.

12. Each student should do (his or her, their) own work.

13. I lost (my, our) favorite earring at the dance.

14. Each woman takes (her, their) own equipment on the camping trip.

15. Each one has a right to (his or her, their) own opinion in this matter.

16. (His, Her) sense of humor is what I like best about Joseph.

17. Some man has left (his, their) raincoat.

18. The two waiters dropped (his, their) trays when they bumped into each other.

19. Has each student received (his or her, their) report card?

20. Every person is expected to do (her or his, their) best.

21. We knew that every man at the meeting expressed (his, their) opinion.

22. Every woman furnishes (her, their) own transportation.

23. Jeff and Tom found (his, their) cabin in the dark.

24. Cliff brings his dog every time (he, she) visits.

25. The bird was in (their, its) nest.

26. Mark read (his, her) final essay for me.

Relative Pronouns

■ A **relative pronoun** is a pronoun that can introduce a subordinate clause. The relative pronouns are <u>who</u>, <u>whom</u>, <u>whose</u> (referring to persons); <u>which</u> (referring to things); and <u>that</u> (referring to persons or things).

■ A **subordinate clause**, when introduced by a relative pronoun, serves as an adjective. It modifies a word, or antecedent, in the main clause.
EXAMPLES: Tom knows the author **whose** articles we read in class. The family for **whom** I work is from Canada. The movie **that** won the prize is playing.

■ **Underline each relative pronoun, and circle its antecedent.**

1. The (letter) <u>that</u> was published in our daily paper was very long.

2. It was Karen who sang the most difficult song.

3. Robert Burns, who wrote "My Heart's in the Highlands," was Scottish.

4. It was Sylvia who wanted Zach's address.

5. The shop that was filled with video games is going out of business.

6. My parents live in a New England farmhouse that was built many years ago.

7. This is the pearl that is so valuable.

8. The bridge, which is made of wood, was built two hundred years ago.

9. Did you see the animal that ran across the road?

10. Good roads have opened up many regions that were formerly impassable.

11. For our Thanksgiving dinner, we had a turkey that weighed twenty pounds.

12. This story, which was written by Eudora Welty, is most interesting.

13. Anna is a person whom you can trust.

14. We ate the delicious hamburgers that Andrew had prepared.

15. Food that is eaten in pleasant surroundings is usually digested easily.

16. This is the first painting that I did.

17. The sweater that you want is too expensive.

18. She is the one whom we watched at the track meet.

19. The only money that they spent was for food.

20. Your friend is one person who is inconsiderate.

21. A rare animal that lives in our city zoo was featured on the evening news.

22. Heather is one of the guests whom I invited.

23. Is this the file for which you've been searching?

24. Leonardo da Vinci is the artist whose work they most admire.

25. The science museum is an attraction that is visited by many tourists.

26. Charles Dickens is a writer whom I've read extensively.

Using *Who/Whom*

- Use who as a subject pronoun.   EXAMPLE: **Who** is your favorite rock star?
- Use whom as an object pronoun.   EXAMPLE: **Whom** did Karen call?
  By rearranging the sentence (Karen did call **whom**?), you can see that
  whom follows the verb and functions as the object. It can also function
  as the object of a preposition.   EXAMPLE: For **whom** are you looking?

■ **Complete each sentence with who or whom.**

1. _____ told you about our plans?

2. _____ is our greatest living scientist?

3. _____ did Armando send for?

4. _____ are those women?

5. _____ is your instructor?

6. _____ is your friend?

7. To _____ is that package addressed?

8. For _____ shall I ask?

9. _____ do you think can take my place?

10. From _____ did you borrow that costume?

11. _____ have the people elected?

12. _____ does she look like?

13. With _____ do you plan to study?

14. _____ is the new employee?

15. _____ do I resemble, my mother or my father?

16. The person _____ I called is my sister.

17. For _____ is this letter?

18. _____ will we select?

19. _____ told us about Frank?

20. _____ did he call?

21. _____ sat next to me?

Using Pronouns

■ **Underline the correct pronoun.**

1. It was (I, me) who brought the telegram.

2. (He, Him) and (I, me) are friends.

3. She used a sentence (who, that) contained a clause.

4. Neither (he, him) nor (she, her) was to blame.

5. Megan, will you sit between Dana and (I, me)?

6. The person (who, which) taught us how to swim has moved.

7. (Who, Whom) do you want?

8. Between you and (I, me), I do not believe that rumor.

9. I was not the only person (who, whom) she helped.

10. Lupe, please let Carla and (I, me) go with you.

11. For (who, whom) did Joanne knit this sweater?

12. A misunderstanding arose between (she, her) and (I, me).

13. Did you and (she, her) speak to (he, him) about the meeting?

14. The doctor (who, which) examined the sick child was very gentle.

15. That is a fox, and (them, those) are coyotes.

16. Is that (she, her) in your car?

17. Calvin invited Zachary and (I, me) to go swimming.

18. Everyone will write (his or her, their) name.

19. Between you and (I, me), I am disappointed.

20. (Those, That) are my books.

21. Patricia chose you and (I, me).

22. Have you ever played tennis with Brenda and (he, him)?

23. (These, This) are very expensive.

24. It is (he, him) who always plans our refreshments.

25. Were Charles and (he, him) ill yesterday?

26. (Those, That) are the singers we want to hear.

27. Our boss will tell Andy and (I, me).

28. Was it (he, him) who won the prize?

29. The person (who, whom) we met comes from Brazil.

30. Both want (his or her, their) papers.

31. (Who, Whom) walked three miles this morning?

32. Was it (she, her) who called this morning?

33. No one should comb (his or her, their) hair in public.

34. I thanked the woman (who, whom) helped me.

Adjectives

> ■ An **adjective** is a word that modifies a noun or a pronoun.
>   EXAMPLE: He has **red** hair.
> ■ A **descriptive adjective** usually tells **what kind, which one,** or **how many.**
>   EXAMPLES: **dreary** weather, **this** camera, **two** tickets
> ■ A **proper adjective** is an adjective that is formed from a proper noun. It
>   always begins with a capital letter.
>   EXAMPLES: **Swedish** history, **Mexican** food
> ■ The articles a, an, and the are called **limiting adjectives.**

A. Underline each adjective.

1. The old delicatessen sells fabulous Greek pastries.

2. The little dog is a very affectionate pet.

3. The weary traveler lay down upon the soft, green turf.

4. The storm was accompanied with a magnificent display of vivid lightning.

5. Every motorist should have good eyes, good ears, and good judgment.

6. Every child in the United States knows about the famous ride of Paul Revere.

7. Fleecy, white clouds were floating overhead.

8. On every side were lofty peaks.

9. We have many clear, bright days in December.

10. Washington was a person of courage and honor.

11. The beautiful memorial fountain was placed near the main entrance of the city park.

12. Cautious movements are required in dangerous areas.

13. Alaska, with its fertile soil, extensive forests, and valuable mines, is a great state.

14. He has a massive head, a broad, deep brow, and large, black eyes.

15. The rain dashed against the windows with a dreary sound.

16. Exercise should be a part of your daily routine.

17. The main street is bordered by stately elms.

18. Show a friendly attitude toward your classmates.

19. The second seat in the fourth row is broken.

20. The bright, colorful leaves of the maple make a wonderful sight in autumn.

21. The old, dusty books were donated to the library.

22. Yellow and green parrots talked to the curious children.

23. The steaming blueberry pie was set on the table.

24. An elegant woman stepped out of the black limousine.

25. Can you hear the chirping baby robins?

26. The salesperson waited on the first customer in line.

B. Form a proper adjective from each proper noun, and use it in a sentence.

1. Puerto Rico _____

2. Ireland _____

3. South America _____

4. Britain _____

5. France _____

6. Rome _____

7. Canada _____

8. England _____

9. Russia _____

C. Write three adjectives to describe each noun.

1. a friend   _____   _____   _____

2. a TV program   _____   _____   _____

3. a book   _____   _____   _____

4. a sunset   _____   _____   _____

5. a conversation   _____   _____   _____

6. a soldier   _____   _____   _____

7. a party   _____   _____   _____

8. a pet   _____   _____   _____

9. a child   _____   _____   _____

10. a tree   _____   _____   _____

D. Write two adjectives that could be substituted for the following common adjectives.

1. pretty   _____   _____

2. little   _____   _____

3. smart   _____   _____

4. big   _____   _____

5. nice   _____   _____

6. good   _____   _____

Demonstrative Adjectives

- A **demonstrative adjective** is one that points out a specific person or thing.
- This and that modify singular nouns. This points to a person or thing nearby, and that points to a person or thing farther away.
    EXAMPLES: **This** pasta is delicious! **That** road will lead us to town.
- These and those describe plural nouns. These points to people or things nearby, and those points to people or things farther away.
    EXAMPLES: **These** sunglasses are very stylish. **Those** plants grow well in shady areas.
- The word them is a pronoun. Never use it to describe a noun.

- **Underline the correct word.**

1. Please hand me one of (those, them) pencils.

2. Who are (those, them) people?

3. Was your report made from (these, them) articles?

4. Have you heard (those, them) harmonica players?

5. (These, Them) ten problems are very difficult.

6. I do not like (that, those) loud music.

7. I like (this, these) kind of soft lead pencil.

8. (Those, Them) shoes are too small for you.

9. Where did you buy (those, them) cantaloupes?

10. Most people like (that, those) kind of mystery story.

11. Please look carefully for (those, them) receipts.

12. Sylvia, please take your brother (these, them) books.

13. (Those, Them) advertisements are very confusing.

14. (Those, Them) buildings are not open to the public.

15. Where did you find (that, those) uniform?

16. Please seat (these, them) guests.

17. Rich lives in (this, these) building.

18. (Those, Them) actors were exceptionally convincing in their roles.

19. Kelly, I sent you (that, these) brochure you requested.

20. Did you see (this, those) new outfits in the store?

21. Mark and Melissa painted (this, these) scenery.

22. (Those, Them) computer programs have been quite helpful.

23. Anna, would you like to read (these, them) memos?

24. (This, These) pair of sandals feels comfortable.

25. Is (that, those) the correct phone number?

Name _____   Date _____

Comparing with Adjectives

- An adjective has three degrees of comparison: **positive, comparative,** and **superlative.**
- The simple form of an adjective is called the **positive** degree.
    EXAMPLE: Cornell is **happy.**
- When two people or things are being compared, the **comparative** degree is used.
    EXAMPLE: Cornell is **happier** than Katya.
- When three or more people or things are being compared, the **superlative** degree is used.
    EXAMPLE: Cornell is the **happiest** person I know.
- For all adjectives of one syllable and a few adjectives of two syllables, add -er to form the comparative degree and -est to form the superlative degree.
    EXAMPLE: tall—taller—tallest
- For some adjectives of two syllables, and all adjectives of three or more syllables, use more or less to form the comparative and most or least to form the superlative.
    EXAMPLES: He is **more** educated than I remember. That is the **most** beautiful horse on the farm. Yoko is **less** active than Mason. Brooke is the **least** active of all.
- Some adjectives have irregular comparisons.
    EXAMPLES: good, better, best   bad, worse, worst

A. Write the comparative and superlative forms of each adjective.

POSITIVE	COMPARATIVE	SUPERLATIVE
1. gentle	_____	_____
2. helpful	_____	_____
3. difficult	_____	_____
4. troublesome	_____	_____
5. high	_____	_____
6. delicious	_____	_____
7. intelligent	_____	_____
8. soft	_____	_____

B. Complete each sentence, using the correct degree of comparison for each adjective in parentheses.

1. (difficult)   This is the _____ problem I have ever faced.

2. (lovely)   A rose is _____ than its thorns.

3. (agreeable)   Ann is _____ in the morning than in the evening.

Adverbs

■ An **adverb** is a word that modifies a verb, an adjective, or another adverb.
   EXAMPLES: Kevin spoke **casually.** Carmen's attitude is **very** positive.
   We did the job **too** carelessly.
■ An adverb usually tells **how, when, where, to what extent,** or **how often.**
■ Many adverbs end in -<u>ly</u>.

■ **Underline each adverb in the sentences below.**

1. Preventive medicine has advanced rapidly.

2. The surface of the lake is very quiet.

3. Slowly and surely the tortoise won the race.

4. Afterward the child slept soundly.

5. Tom Sawyer's fence was carefully and thoroughly whitewashed.

6. The horse ran gracefully through the woods.

7. Slowly but steadily the river rose.

8. Jane, you read too rapidly.

9. Liz always dresses stylishly and neatly.

10. The driver turned quickly and abruptly.

11. Was the firefighter seriously injured?

12. Cynthia was extremely cautious as she moved slowly away from the danger.

13. Always try to speak correctly and clearly.

14. The assistant typed rapidly.

15. She came in very quietly.

16. Julio worked patiently and carefully.

17. We searched everywhere.

18. Our holidays passed too quickly.

19. The giant airplane landed gently.

20. We looked here, there, and everywhere for Sue's lost ring.

21. Come here immediately!

22. The flags were waving gaily everywhere.

23. Slowly the long freight train climbed the steep grade.

24. Overhead the stars twinkled brightly.

25. Wash your hands thoroughly before eating.

26. Scott caught the ball and speedily passed it to his teammate.

27. Carefully check every belt and hose in the car.

28. They were quite late.

29. He sees too many movies.

Comparing with Adverbs

- An **adverb** has three degrees of comparison: **positive, comparative,** and **superlative.**
- The simple form of the adverb is called the **positive** degree.
    EXAMPLE: Alex worked **hard** on his project.
- When two actions are being compared, the **comparative** degree is used.
    EXAMPLE: Alex worked **harder** than Justin.
- When three or more actions are being compared, the **superlative** degree is used.
    EXAMPLE: Alex worked the **hardest** of all.
- Use -er to form the comparative degree, and use -est to form the superlative degree of one-syllable adverbs.
- Use more and most with longer adverbs and with adverbs that end in ly.
    EXAMPLE: Karen finished **more quickly** than Sally. Sally works the **most carefully** of the two.
- Some adverbs have irregular comparative and superlative degrees.
    EXAMPLES: well, better, best   badly, worse, worst

A. Write the comparative and superlative form of each adverb.

POSITIVE	COMPARATIVE	SUPERLATIVE
1. fast	_____	_____
2. carefully	_____	_____
3. quietly	_____	_____
4. slow	_____	_____
5. frequently	_____	_____
6. proudly	_____	_____
7. evenly	_____	_____
8. long	_____	_____

B. Complete each sentence using the correct degree of comparison for each adverb in parentheses. Some of the forms are irregular.

1. (seriously) Does Angela take her job _____ than Beth?

2. (high) Which of the kites flew _____ ?

3. (thoroughly) Who cleaned his plate _____ , Juan or Bruce?

4. (badly) This is the _____ I've ever done on a test.

5. (diligently) Carl works _____ than Mario!

6. (well) Lisa skis the _____ of everyone in her family.

Name _____ Date _____

Using Adjectives and Adverbs

■ **Underline the correct word.**

1. Always drive very (careful, carefully).

2. The lake seems (calm, calmly) today.

3. The storm raged (furious, furiously).

4. The dog waited (patient, patiently) for its owner.

5. Nicole's letters are always (cheerful, cheerfully) written.

6. Although our team played (good, well), we lost the game.

7. Always answer your mail (prompt, promptly).

8. James speaks (respectful, respectfully) to everyone.

9. Tara is (happy, happily) with her new work.

10. Write this address (legible, legibly).

11. The time passed (slow, slowly).

12. The robin chirped (happy, happily) from its nest.

13. We were (sure, surely) glad to hear from him.

14. Rebecca tries to do her work (good, well).

15. I think Brenda will (easy, easily) win that contest.

16. We had to talk (loud, loudly) to be heard.

17. Yesterday the sun shone (bright, brightly) all day.

18. He says he sleeps (good, well) every night.

19. The elevator went up (quick, quickly) to the top floor.

20. The storm began very (sudden, suddenly).

21. You did react very (cautious, cautiously).

22. Every student should do this work (accurate, accurately).

23. Eric rode his bike (furious, furiously) to get home on time.

24. The paint on the house is (new, newly).

25. The mist fell (steady, steadily) all evening.

26. The river looked (beautiful, beautifully) in the moonlight.

27. The salesperson always answers questions (courteous, courteously).

28. He always does (good, well) when selling that product.

29. Ryan can swim (good, well).

30. I was (real, really) excited about going to San Francisco.

31. I think he talks (foolish, foolishly).

32. It seems (foolish, foolishly) to me.

33. That bell rang too (loud, loudly) for this small room.

34. Our grass seems to grow very (rapid, rapidly).

Prepositions and Prepositional Phrases

- A **preposition** is a word that shows the relationship of a noun or a pronoun to another word in the sentence.
  EXAMPLES: I saw her coming **around** the **corner.**
  She placed the present **on** the **chair.**
- These are some commonly used prepositions:

about	against	at	between	from	of	through	until
above	along	before	by	in	off	to	up
across	among	behind	down	into	on	toward	upon
after	around	beneath	for	near	over	under	with

- A **prepositional phrase** is a group of words that begins with a preposition and ends with a noun or pronoun.
  EXAMPLE: We borrowed the lawn mower **from Ken.**
- The noun or pronoun in the prepositional phrase is called the **object of the preposition.**
  EXAMPLE: Megan hurried **down** the **stairs.**

■ **Underline each prepositional phrase. Then circle each preposition.**

1. Salt Lake City, Utah's capital and largest city, was founded (in) 1847.
2. Sir Authur Conan Doyle is famous for creating the beloved detective Sherlock Holmes.
3. Standard time was adopted in the United States in 1884.
4. The geographic center of the United States is in Kansas.
5. The first safety lamp for miners was invented by Sir Humphrey Davy in 1816.
6. Many people of North Borneo live in houses that have been built on stilts in the Brunei River.
7. The children were charmed by the magician's tricks.
8. We visited the Royal Ontario Museum in Canada.
9. The first automobile show was held in New York City in 1900.
10. Self-government in the United States began in Jamestown in 1619.
11. The first street railway in the world was built in New York in 1832.
12. The inventor of the telephone was born in Scotland.
13. Who is the inventor of the printing press?
14. The shadowy outline of the giant skyscrapers loomed before us.
15. Our small boat bobbed in the waves.
16. The swivel chair was invented by Thomas Jefferson.
17. A raging storm fell upon the quiet valley.
18. I was lulled to sleep by the patter of the rain.
19. We found acorns beneath the tree.
20. That cow is standing in the middle of the road.
21. The child ran across the yard and around the tree.
22. A pine tree fell across the brook.

78

23. The first census of our country was taken in 1790.

24. Tons of violets are made into perfume each year.

25. The heart of a person pumps more than four quarts of blood in one minute.

26. The United States Patent Office was established in 1836.

27. One of the secrets of success is the wise use of leisure time.

28. The school board held its annual banquet at this hotel.

29. Duke Ellington was born in Washington, D.C.

30. Deposits of iron ore exist near the western end of the Great Lakes.

31. The bridge across this stream was destroyed by the recent storm.

32. Many herds of cattle once grazed on these plains.

33. The huddle in football was first used by a team from Georgia University in 1896.

34. The first skyscraper was built in Chicago.

35. Travelers of a century ago journeyed by stagecoach.

36. The tower of Delhi in India is a monument to the skill of its builders.

37. The quiet of the evening was broken by the rumbling of thunder.

38. The parachutist was injured when her parachute caught in a tree.

39. Aviation was born on a sand dune in North Carolina in 1903.

40. The first trolley car was installed in Richmond in 1885.

41. A box of rusty nails was in the corner of the garage.

42. Don't stand near the edge of that steep cliff.

43. The ground was covered with a deep snow.

44. Twenty cars were involved in the accident on the expressway.

45. The study of geography teaches us about the layout of other lands.

46. A thin column of smoke rose from the chimney of the cabin.

47. In the distance, we saw the top of the snow-capped peak.

48. Place the book upon the shelf.

49. At one time, Philadelphia was the capital of the United States.

50. The football sailed between the goal posts.

51. The report of the secretary was given at the beginning of the meeting.

52. A group of cheering fans waited at the entrance.

53. The hot air balloon drifted toward the ground.

54. Let's have our picnic beneath this huge tree.

55. In the glow of the fading light, we drove along the road.

56. Emily lives near the new mall.

57. Look in the card catalog to see if this book is in the library.

58. The tour guide led us through the halls of the mansion.

59. The theater group is meeting to discuss its productions for next year.

Conjunctions

> - A **conjunction** is a word used to join words or groups of words.
>   EXAMPLE: Jenna **and** her sister are in Arizona.
> - These are some commonly used conjunctions:
>
> | although | because | however | or | that | when | while |
> |----------|---------|---------|-----|-------|---------|-------|
> | and | but | if | since | though | whereas | yet |
> | as | for | nor | than | unless | whether | |
>
> - Some conjunctions are used in pairs. These include either . . .or, neither . . . nor, and not only . . . but also.

■ **Underline each conjunction.**

1. He and I are friends.

2. David likes tennis, whereas Jim prefers running.

3. We had to wait since it was raining.

4. We left early, but we missed the train.

5. The show was not only long but also boring.

6. Neither the chairs nor the tables had been dusted.

7. Hail and sleet fell during the storm.

8. Neither Carmen nor Kara was able to attend the meeting.

9. I have neither time nor energy to waste.

10. Bowling and tennis are my favorite sports.

11. Either Dan or Don will bring a portable radio.

12. The people in the car and the people in the van exchanged greetings.

13. Neither cookies nor cake is on your diet.

14. Although I like to take photographs, I am not a good photographer.

15. Did you see Charles when he visited here?

16. We are packing our bags since our vacation trip begins tomorrow.

17. She cannot concentrate while you are making so much noise.

18. Unless you hurry, the party will be over before you arrive.

19. We enjoyed the visit although we were very tired.

20. Both mammals and birds are warm-blooded.

21. She is one performer who can both sing and dance.

22. Unless you have some objections, I will submit this report.

23. Neither dogs nor cats are allowed in this park.

24. April watered the plants while Luis mowed the lawn.

25. I will see you when you are feeling better.

26. Either Ms. Andretti or Ms. Garcia will teach that course.

27. We got here late because we lost our directions.

Double Negatives

■ The **adverbs** <u>not</u>, <u>never</u>, <u>hardly</u>, <u>scarcely</u>, <u>seldom</u>, <u>none</u>, and <u>nothing</u> should not be used with a negative verb. One clause cannot properly contain two negatives.

    EXAMPLES: There wasn't anything left in the refrigerator. (Correct)
There wasn't nothing left in the refrigerator. (Incorrect)

■ **Underline the correct word.**

1. We couldn't see (anything, nothing) through the fog.

2. The suspect wouldn't admit (anything, nothing).

3. I don't know (any, none) of the people on this bus.

4. Rosa couldn't do (anything, nothing) about changing the time of our program.

5. We didn't have (any, no) printed programs.

6. I don't want (any, no) cereal for breakfast this morning.

7. You must not speak to (anyone, no one) about our surprise party plans.

8. There isn't (any, no) ink in this pen.

9. Didn't you make (any, no) copies for the other people?

10. I haven't had (any, no) time to repair the lawn mower.

11. She hasn't said (anything, nothing) about her accident.

12. Hardly (anything, nothing) pleases him.

13. There aren't (any, no) pears in this supermarket.

14. There isn't (any, no) newspaper in that little town.

15. There wasn't (anybody, nobody) in the house.

16. Please don't ask him (any, no) questions.

17. I haven't solved (any, none) of my problems.

18. I haven't done (anything, nothing) to offend Greg.

19. We don't have (any, no) water pressure.

20. Our team wasn't (any, no) match for the opposing team.

21. I couldn't hear (anything, nothing) because of the airplane's noise.

22. The salesperson didn't have (any, no) samples on display.

23. I haven't (any, no) money with me.

24. Hasn't he cooked (any, none) of the pasta?

25. We haven't (any, no) more packages to wrap.

26. Wasn't there (anyone, no one) at home?

27. My dog has never harmed (anybody, nobody).

28. They seldom have (anyone, no one) absent from their meetings.

29. There weren't (any, no) clouds in the sky.

Unit 3 Test

Choose (A) if the noun is abstract, (B) if it is concrete, or (C) if it is collective.

1. scissors   A ○   B ○   C ○   4. pride   A ○   B ○   C ○

2. team   A ○   B ○   C ○   5. wastebasket   A ○   B ○   C ○

3. fruit   A ○   B ○   C ○   6. happiness   A ○   B ○   C ○

Choose (A) if the noun is singular, (B) if it is plural, or (C) if it is possessive.

7. Jason's   A ○   B ○   C ○   10. woman's   A ○   B ○   C ○

8. flies   A ○   B ○   C ○   11. pumpkin   A ○   B ○   C ○

9. geese   A ○   B ○   C ○   12. ribbon   A ○   B ○   C ○

Choose the sentence in which the appositive is underlined.

13. **A** ○ Her oldest daughter, Emily, won the debate.

     B ○ Bill serves as a volunteer firefighter, in addition to being a reporter.

     C ○ "Why," asked Mary, "did you pretend to be gone?"

     D ○ Mayor Shea, our new mayor, has spent years in public service.

Choose the sentence in which the antecedent is underlined.

14. **A** ○ Every contestant did his or her best.

     B ○ The planets revolve around the sun in their orbits.

     C ○ Most of the employees have taken their vacations.

     D ○ George finished his work early and went to the lake.

Choose (A) if the underlined word(s) is an infinitive, (B) if it is a gerund, or (C) if it is a participle.

15. Jeff wants to go after school.   A ○   B ○   C ○

16. The bubbling brook was a beautiful sight.   A ○   B ○   C ○

17. Helping others is very rewarding.   A ○   B ○   C ○

18. Don't forget to write to me while you're away.   A ○   B ○   C ○

19. Baked pumpkin seeds are delicious.   A ○   B ○   C ○

20. Dan's hobby is building model airplanes.   A ○   B ○   C ○

Choose the correct verb to complete each sentence.

21. I had _____ to see the new baby.   **A** ○ came   **B** ○ coming   **C** ○ come

22. Marie _____ blood at the health center.   **A** ○ gave   **B** ○ given   **C** ○ give

23. Luis is _____ some vegetables in his garden.   **A** ○ grew   **B** ○ grown   **C** ○ growing

24. My brother has _____ a military jet.   **A** ○ flown   **B** ○ flying   **C** ○ flew

25. They are _____ in the race today.   **A** ○ swimming   **B** ○ swam   **C** ○ swim

26. Jason _____ his winter coat to the game.   **A** ○ wore   **B** ○ worn   **C** ○ wearing

27. He has _____ awake for hours.   **A** ○ laid   **B** ○ lain   **C** ○ layed

28. Please _____ me to sew.   **A** ○ teach   **B** ○ learn   **C** ○ teaching

29. It is _____ to get cloudy.   **A** ○ begin   **B** ○ beginning   **C** ○ began

30. Did you _____ that iced tea?   **A** ○ drank   **B** ○ drunk   **C** ○ drink

31. Just _____ the books there.   **A** ○ lie   **B** ○ lay   **C** ○ laid

32. I'll _____ here to rest.   **A** ○ set   **B** ○ sit   **C** ○ sat

Choose the sentence in which pronouns are used correctly.

33. **A** ○ We hoped the winning contestant was her.

    B ○ The woman for whom we gave the party was delighted.

    C ○ The dog licked it's paw after stepping on the thistle.

    D ○ He went to the store with Hoan and I.

34. **A** ○ The elephant uses its trunk to drink water.

    B ○ William and Todd played his guitars.

    C ○ Janice and me chose the same restaurant.

    D ○ He said it was them who took it.

35. **A** ○ Whom broke this vase?

    B ○ The new house is their.

    C ○ Elena and she tied for first place.

    D ○ It couldn't have been them.

36. **A** ○ Did him answer the phone?

    B ○ Between you and I, I think it's wrong.

    C ○ Dirk is me younger brother.

    D ○ Whom did you ask first?

Choose the correct adjective or adverb to complete each sentence.

37. This book is the _____ I have ever read.   **A** ○ more interesting   **B** ○ most interesting   **C** ○ interesting

38. I can run _____ in my new shoes.   **A** ○ more quick   **B** ○ more quicker   **C** ○ more quickly

39. Where did you find _____ shoes?   **A** ○ them   **B** ○ those   **C** ○ that

Choose the sentence that has the prepositional phrase underlined.

40. **A** ○ I didn't want to trust her at the beginning.

    B ○ The house on the hill was completely destroyed by fire.

    C ○ In the early evening, the moon came out.

    D ○ Throw down the blanket, please.

Using Capital Letters

- **Capitalize** the first word of a sentence and of each line of poetry.
  EXAMPLES: Maria wrote a poem. It began as follows:
  One cold, starry night
  I saw the stars taking flight.
- Capitalize all proper nouns.
  EXAMPLES: Ellen Kennan, Uncle John, First Street, Spain, Virginia, White Mountains, New Year's Day, March, Niles High School, *Sea Voyager*
- Capitalize the first word of a quotation.
  EXAMPLE: Tonya said, "Everyone should learn a poem."
- Capitalize the first, last, and all important words in the titles of books, poems, stories, and songs.
  EXAMPLES: "Somewhere Over the Rainbow"; *The Call of the Wild*
- Capitalize all proper adjectives. A proper adjective is an adjective that is made from a proper noun.
  EXAMPLES: the French language, German food, American tourists

A. Circle each letter that should be capitalized. Write the capital letter above it.

1. henry wadsworth longfellow wove the history of america into his poems

   "evangeline" and "the courtship of miles standish."

2. "the midnight ride of paul revere" is another of longfellow's poems.

3. The british ship *titanic* sank on its first trip from england to the united states.

4. the first law course offered by an american college was taught by george wythe.

5. he taught many famous people, including thomas jefferson and james monroe.

6. The mississippi river flows through vicksburg, mississippi, and new orleans, louisiana.

7. "what time do the church bells ring?" asked amelia.

8. robert answered, "i believe they ring every half hour."

9. Many centuries ago, vikings lived in what is now known as norway, sweden, and denmark.

10. the song "the battle hymn of the republic" was written by julia ward howe.

11. Mr. james nelson lives in chicago, illinois.

12. he asked, "have you ever seen a waterfall?"

13. The president of the united states lives in the white house.

14. Last summer I visited a hopi reservation.

15. The sequoia national park is on the western slope of the sierra nevada mountains in california.

> - Capitalize a person's title when it comes before a name.
>   EXAMPLES: Doctor Lerner, Judge Kennedy, Governor Thompson
> - Capitalize abbreviations of titles.
>   EXAMPLES: Mr. J. D. Little, Dr. Simon, Pres. Clinton

B. Circle each letter that should be capitalized. Write the capital letter above it.

1. mayor jones and senator small attended the awards banquet Friday night.

2. dr. fox is a veterinarian at the local animal hospital.

3. The invitation said to respond to ms. hilary johnson.

4. No one expected judge randall to rule in favor of the defendant.

5. We were disappointed that gov. dickson couldn't speak at graduation.

6. In his place will be senator christopher larson.

7. The speaker will be introduced by supt. adams.

8. Will miss alden be the new history instructor?

9. dr. tabor is a surgeon at Parkside Hospital.

10. His first patient was mr. william benton.

> - Capitalize abbreviations of days and months, parts of addresses, and titles of members of the armed forces. Also capitalize all letters in the abbreviations of states.
>   EXAMPLES: Fri.; Aug.; 267 N. Concord Ave.; Col. Fernando Gonzales; Hartford, CT; Athens, GA

C. Circle each letter that should be capitalized. Write the capital letter above it.

1. When is maj. hanson expected back from his trip overseas?

2. The garage sale is at 101 w. charles st.

3. Have you ever been to orlando, fl?

4. There is a house for sale at the corner of maple ave. and sunset st.

5. Everyone in our company has the first mon. off in september for Labor Day.

6. The highest award for service was given to gen. t. j. quint.

7. The letter from memphis, tn, took only two days to arrive.

8. Did you know that col. kravitz will be stationed in dover, nh?

9. His address will be 1611 falmouth harbor, dover, nh 03805.

Using End Punctuation

> ■ Use a **period** at the end of a declarative sentence.
>   EXAMPLE: We are going to Mexico on our vacation.
> ■ Use a **question mark** at the end of an interrogative sentence.
>   EXAMPLE: Do you know whose picture is on the one-dollar bill?

A. Use a period or question mark to end each sentence below.

1. Does this road wind uphill all the way to Carol's house____

2. Los Angeles, Mexico City, and Rome have all been sites of the Olympic Games____

3. Were there really one hundred people standing in line at the theater____

4. Wisconsin raises hay, corn, and oats____

5. Pablo, Tom, Carlos, and Ling were nominated as candidates____

6. Whom did you see, Elizabeth____

7. Haydn, Mozart, Mendelssohn, and Beethoven composed symphonies____

8. Hummingbirds and barn swallows migrate____

9. Do you think that Napoleon was an able leader____

10. Does Louise live in Los Angeles, California____

11. Who wrote the Declaration of Independence____

12. We flew from Seattle, Washington, to Miami, Florida____

13. Roy Avery is a guest of Mr. and Mrs. Benson____

14. Anna, have you read "The Gift of the Magi" by O. Henry____

B. Add the correct end punctuation where needed in the paragraphs below.

Have you ever heard of Harriet Tubman and the Underground Railroad____ During the Civil War in the United States, Harriet Tubman, a former slave, helped more than three hundred slaves escape to freedom____ Tubman led slaves on the dangerous route of the Underground Railroad____ It was not actually a railroad but a series of secret homes and shelters that led through the South to the free North and Canada____ How dangerous was her work____ There were large rewards offered by slaveholders for her capture____ But Tubman was never caught____ She said proudly, "I never lost a passenger____ " She was called the Moses of her people____

During the war, she worked as a spy for the Union army____ An excellent guide, she would lead soldiers into enemy camps____ She also served as a nurse and cook for the soldiers____ She was well respected among leading abolitionists of the time____ She was also a strong supporter of women's rights____

Do you know what she did after the war____ She settled in Auburn, New York, and took care of her parents and any other needy black person____ She was always low on money but never refused anyone____ Later, she set up a home for poor African Americans____

> - Use a **period** at the end of an imperative sentence.
>   EXAMPLE: Please answer the telephone.
> - Use an **exclamation point** at the end of an exclamatory sentence and after an interjection that shows strong feeling. If a command expresses great excitement, use an exclamation point at the end of the sentence.
>   EXAMPLES: Ouch! Follow that car! The ringing is so loud! My ears hurt!

C. Add periods or exclamation points where needed in each sentence below.

1. I love to hike in the mountains____
2. Just look at the view in the distance____
3. Be sure to wear the right kind of shoes____
4. Ouch____ My blister is killing me____
5. Talk quietly and walk softly____
6. Don't scare away the wildlife____
7. Look____ It's a bald eagle____
8. I can't believe how big it is____
9. Take a picture before it flies away____
10. Its wings are bigger than I had ever imagined____
11. It's one of the most breathtaking sights I've ever seen____
12. Oh, look this way____ Here comes another one____
13. This is the luckiest day of my life____
14. Sit down on that tree stump____
15. Pick another place to sit____

D. Add the correct end punctuation where needed in the paragraphs below.

Which animal do you think has been on Earth longer, the dog or the cat____ If you answered the cat, you're right____ About 5,000 years ago in Egypt, cats became accepted household pets____ That was a long time ago____ Cats were actually worshipped in ancient Egypt____

The different members of the cat family have certain things in common____ House cats and wild cats all walk on the tips of their toes____ Isn't that incredible____ Even though all cats don't like water, they can all swim____ Another thing that all cats have in common is a keen hunting ability____ Part of this is due to their eyesight____ They see well at night and in dim light____ Did you know that the cat is the only animal that purrs____ A cat uses its whiskers to feel____ Its sense of touch is located in its whiskers____ The coat of a cat can be long-haired or short-haired, solid-colored or striped____ Some cats even have spots____ Can you name any types of cats____

Name _____   Date _____

Using Commas

> ■ Use a **comma** between words or groups of words that are in a series.
> EXAMPLE: Colorado, Canadian, Ohio, Mississippi, and Missouri are names of well-known American rivers.
> ■ Use a comma before a conjunction in a compound sentence.
> EXAMPLE: Once the rivers were used mainly for transportation, but today they are used for recreation and industry.
> ■ Use a comma after a subordinate clause when it begins a sentence.
> EXAMPLE: When I got to the theater, the movie had already begun.

A. Add commas where needed in the sentences below.

1. Anita Travis and José went to the tennis tournament.

2. Before they found their seats the first match had already begun.

3. It was a close game and they weren't disappointed by the final score.

4. They had come to cheer for Antonio Fergas and he was the winner.

5. Although his opponent was very good Fergas never missed returning a serve.

6. While they watched the match Anita clapped cheered and kept score.

7. Travis and José watched a number of different matches but Anita followed Fergas.

8. He was signing autographs and Anita was first in line.

9. Antonio asked her name signed a tennis ball and shook her hand.

10. Because they enjoyed the match so much Travis José and Anita made plans to come back for the final match the next day.

11. They planned to see the men's women's and doubles' finals.

12. Fergas won the entire tournament and he became the youngest champion in the history of the tournament.

> ■ Use a comma to set off a quotation from the rest of the sentence.
> EXAMPLES: "We'd better leave early," said Travis.
> Travis said, "We'd better leave early."
> ■ Use two commas to set off a divided quotation. Do not capitalize the first word of the second part of the quotation.
> EXAMPLE: "We'd better leave," Travis said, "or we'll be stuck in traffic."

B. Add commas to the quotations below.

1. "The first match starts at 9:00 A.M." said Travis.

2. Anita asked "Do you want to get seats in the same section as yesterday?"

3. "That's fine with me" said José.

4. José said "Fergas's first match is in Court B."

5. "I'll bring the binoculars" said Anita "and you can bring the cooler."

- Use a comma to set off the name of a person who is being addressed.
    EXAMPLE: Philip, would you like to leave now?
- Use a comma to set off words like <u>yes</u>, <u>no</u>, <u>well</u>, <u>oh</u>, <u>first</u>, <u>next</u>, and <u>finally</u> at the beginning of a sentence.
    EXAMPLE: Well, we better get going.
- Use a comma to set off an appositive.
    EXAMPLE: Alan, Philip's brother, is a doctor in Saint Louis.

C. Add commas where needed in the sentences below.

1. Dr. Perillo a nutritionist is an expert on proper eating.

2. "Students it's important to eat a well-balanced diet," she said.

3. "Yes but how do we know what the right foods are?" asked one student.

4. "First you need to look carefully at your eating habits," said Dr. Perillo.

5. "Yes you will keep a journal of the foods you eat," she said.

6. "Dr. Perillo what do you mean by the right servings?" asked Emilio.

7. "Okay good question," she said.

8. "A serving Emilio is a certain amount of a food," said Dr. Perillo.

9. "Dave a cross-country runner will need more calories than a less active student," explained Dr. Perillo.

10. "Class remember to eat foods from the five basic food groups," she said.

D. Add commas where needed in the paragraphs below.

Our neighbor Patrick has fruit trees on his property. "Patrick what kinds of fruit do you grow?" I asked. "Well I grow peaches apricots pears and plums" he replied. "Wow! That's quite a variety" I said. Patrick's son Jonathan helps his dad care for the trees. "Oh it's constant work and care" Jonathan said "but the delicious results are worth the effort." After harvesting the fruit Jonathan's mother Allison cans the fruit for use throughout the year. She makes preserves and she gives them as gifts for special occasions. Allison sells some of her preserves to Chris Simon the owner of a local shop. People come from all over the county to buy Allison's preserves.

Jonathan's aunt Christina grows corn tomatoes beans and squash in her garden. Each year she selects her best vegetables and enters them in the fair. She has won blue ribbons medals and certificates for her vegetables. "Oh I just like being outside. That's why I enjoy gardening" Christina said. Christina's specialty squash-and-tomato bread is one of the most delicious breads I have ever tasted.

Using Quotation Marks and Apostrophes

> ■ Use **quotation marks** to show the exact words of a speaker. Use a comma or another punctuation mark to separate the quotation from the rest of the sentence. A quotation may be placed at the beginning or at the end of a sentence. Begin the quote with a capital letter. Be sure to include all the speaker's words within the quotation marks.
> EXAMPLES: "Let's go to the movie," said Sharon.
> "What time," asked Mark, "does the movie begin?"

A. Add quotation marks and other punctuation where needed in the sentences below.

1. Mary, do you think this is Christine's pen asked Heather.

2. Heather said I don't know. It looks like the kind she uses.

3. Well, I think it's out of ink, Mary replied.

4. Have you seen Barbara's car? asked Sandy.

5. No said Beth, I haven't gotten over to her apartment this week.

6. Sandy said It sure is pretty. I can't wait to ride in it.

7. I can't believe how late it is exclaimed Alan.

8. Paul asked Where are you going on vacation this summer?

9. My brother and I are visiting our parents in Maine said Peter.

10. Tell me, Alison said how many cats do you have?

11. Alison said The last time we counted, there were four.

12. Will you be taking the bus home asked James or do you need a ride?

> ■ Use an **apostrophe** in a contraction to show where a letter or letters have been taken out.
> EXAMPLE: **Let's** go to the store. I **can't** go until tomorrow.
> ■ Use an apostrophe to form a possessive noun. Add -'s to most singular nouns. Add -' to most plural nouns. Add -'s to a few nouns that have irregular plurals.
> EXAMPLES: **Maria's** sons are musicians. The **sons'** voices are magnificent. They sing in a **children's** choir.

B. Write the words in which an apostrophe has been left out. Insert apostrophes where they are needed.

1. Im sorry I cant make it to the concert. _____ _____

2. I cant go until Beths project is completed. _____ _____

3. Ill need two nights notice. _____ _____

4. Ive heard that the bandleaders favorite piece will be played last. _____ _____

5. Isnt it one of Cole Porters songs? _____ _____

Using Colons and Semicolons

> - Use a **colon** after the greeting in a business letter.
>   EXAMPLES: Dear Mrs. Miller: Dear Sirs:
> - Use a colon between the hour and the minutes when writing the time.
>   EXAMPLES: 11:45   3:30   9:10
> - Use a colon to introduce a list.
>   EXAMPLE: The shopping cart contained the following items: milk, eggs, crackers, apples, soap, and paper towels.

A. Add colons where needed in the sentences below.

1. At 9 1 0 this morning, we'll be leaving for the natural history museum.

2. Please bring the following materials with you pencils, paper, erasers, and a notebook.

3. The bus will be back at 4 0 0 to pick us up.

4. The special exhibit on birds contains the following types prehistoric birds, sea birds, and domestic birds.

5. The letter we wrote to the museum began "Dear Sir Please let us know when the special exhibition on penguins will be shown at your museum."

6. He told us that we could find out more about the following kinds of penguins the Emperor, the Adélie, and the Magellan.

7. We were afraid there would be so much to see that we wouldn't be ready to leave at 3 3 0 when the museum closed.

> - Use a **semicolon** between the clauses of a compound sentence that are closely related but not connected by a conjunction. Do not capitalize the word after a semicolon.
>   EXAMPLE: Hummingbirds and barn swallows migrate; most sparrows live in one place all year.

B. Rewrite each sentence below, adding semicolons where needed.

1. Colleen is a clever teacher she is also an inspiring one.

   _____

2. Her lectures are interesting they are full of information.

   _____

3. She has a college degree in history world history is her specialty.

   _____

4. She begins her classes by answering questions she ends them by asking questions.

   _____

Using Other Punctuation

> ■ Use a **hyphen** between the parts of some compound words.
>   EXAMPLE: poverty-stricken   sixty-three   two-thirds
>   part-time   able-bodied   brother-in-law
>   hard-boiled   short-term   red-hot
> ■ Use a hyphen to separate the syllables of a word that is carried over from one line to the next.
>   EXAMPLE: So many things were going on at once that no one could pos-sibly guess how the play would end.

A. Add hyphens where needed in the sentences below.

1. The director told us that there would be room for only two busloads, or eighty four people.

2. The play was going to be in an old fashioned theater.

3. Between acts the theater was completely dark, but the orchestra con tinued to play anyway.

4. The theater was so small that there were seats for only ninety two people.

5. The vice president was played by Alan Lowe.

> ■ Use a **dash** to set off words that interrupt the main thought of a sentence or to show a sudden change of thought.
>   EXAMPLES: We were surprised—even shocked—by the news.
>   It was Wednesday—no it was Friday—that I was sick.

B. Add dashes where needed in the sentences below.

1. There was a loud boom what a fright from the back of the theater.

2. We all turned around I even jumped up to see what it was.

3. It was part of the play imagine that meant to add suspense.

4. I'd love to see the play again maybe next week and bring Andrea.

> ■ **Underline** the titles of books, plays, magazines, films, and television series.
>   EXAMPLE: We read <u>Romeo and Juliet</u> last term.
> ■ Underline foreign words and phrases.
>   EXAMPLE: "<u>Adieu</u>," said the French actor to his co-star.

C. In the sentences below, underline where needed.

1. We saw the movie Of Mice and Men after we had read the novel.

2. In Spanish, "Hasta la vista" means "See you later."

3. My favorite book is Little Women.

4. I took a copy of Life magazine out of the library.

Unit 4 Test

Choose the word in each sentence that should be capitalized.

1. Was senator Curtis a member of the foreign delegation?

    A ○ senator   **B** ○ member   **C** ○ foreign   **D** ○ delegation

2. The foreign students enjoyed the mexican food.

    A ○ foreign   **B** ○ students   **C** ○ mexican   **D** ○ food

3. Their principal was the author of a book called *Getting to know Your Students.*

    A ○ principal   **B** ○ author   **C** ○ *to*   **D** ○ *know*

4. My uncle has a cabin in detroit, Michigan, by the lake.

    A ○ uncle   **B** ○ cabin   **C** ○ detroit   **D** ○ lake

5. where did the three men and their fathers go on vacation?

    A ○ where   **B** ○ men   **C** ○ fathers   **D** ○ vacation

6. "I will just be a moment," said Kate. "please wait for me."

    A ○ moment   **B** ○ said   **C** ○ please   **D** ○ me

7. The speaker told the audience at Howell auditorium that he was an expert.

    A ○ speaker   **B** ○ audience   **C** ○ auditorium   **D** ○ expert

8. My mother's sister moved to the city and lives at 947 east Westwind Street.

    A ○ mother's   **B** ○ sister   **C** ○ city   **D** ○ east

Choose the sentence in which capitalization is used correctly.

9. **A** ○ The nine planets of our solar system revolve around the sun in elliptical orbits.

    B ○ Jeremy said, "let's go to the exhibit at the Museum of Natural History."

    C ○ I need to go to the library and check out *how to Refinish Furniture the Easy Way.*

    D ○ Corporal Henderson moved his family to White Air Force base.

Choose the sentence in which end punctuation is used correctly.

10. **A** ○ I told you the truth?

    B ○ He went back to the house!

    C ○ What a fantastic idea!

    D ○ Don't be sad?

11. **A** ○ I like to read when the weather is bad?

    B ○ We almost made it on time?

    C ○ Can we help you?

    D ○ Haven't I met you before!

12. **A** ○ Look. There's a rainbow.

    B ○ Snakebites can be dangerous.

    C ○ I'd like to know her name?

    D ○ When will you leave for the lake.

13. **A** ○ Ouch. I burned myself.

    B ○ That's her favorite dessert?

    C ○ Everyone likes ice cream?

    D ○ Take the first exit.

Choose the sentence in which commas are used correctly.

14. **A** ○ I like apples but, Todd doesn't.

    B ○ We have a cat, a dog and a fish at home.

    C ○ How, are you Frank?

    D ○ Renee said, "Yes, I can go!"

16. **A** ○ Before school I saw Sue, Neil and, Dan.

    B ○ "What a surprise, Karen!" shouted Gina.

    C ○ Emily do you like peas, or carrots better?

    D ○ I almost, forgot Miguel!

15. **A** ○ After calling her, did you see Amy?

    B ○ Karen please come, or I'll miss you.

    C ○ My neighbor Mr. Ramos said, "Yes, Jim."

    D ○ They elected Jean, Nina and Jesse.

17. **A** ○ "That's a pretty sweater, Lin" said Selina.

    B ○ When we arrive they'll recognize us, Matt.

    C ○ Pat, my cousin, would like to come.

    D ○ Of course I'd love to see you Justin.

Choose the sentence in which quotation marks are used correctly.

18. **A** ○ "Can you come? Tom said."

    B ○ Andy asked, "Did you see the show?

    C ○ "Yes, I will," answered Jana.

    D ○ "Robyn told us, "Don't step there!

19. **A** ○ "I'd like to go, said Lin."

    B ○ Fran said, "Please" hold this.

    C ○ "Are you Canadian? asked June.

    D ○ Jeff said, "I can't believe it!"

Choose the sentence in which apostrophes are used correctly.

20. **A** ○ Don't leave me here alone.

    B ○ He has'nt arrived yet.

    C ○ That notebook is her's.

    D ○ Forget whats' been said already.

21. **A** ○ The teacher is'nt here yet.

    B ○ Their's is the one on the far left.

    C ○ Voting is every person's right.

    D ○ Shell be back soon with the paper.

Choose the sentence in which colons or semicolons are used correctly.

22. **A** ○ Will Renee be there by: 730?

    B ○ The time is now 1:20.

    C ○ Do you have these items a pencil: and paper?

    D ○ By 200; please be at the station.

23. **A** ○ Please: make a list.

    B ○ We like to visit; museums in Chicago.

    C ○ It was 2:00; but nobody showed up.

    D ○ He's my brother; I'm his sister.

Choose the sentence in which dashes or hyphens are used correctly.

24. **A** ○ Do you like hard boiled-eggs?

    B ○ Tell me—I'm starting it now—how to do this project.

    C ○ I am working-on a short term basis.

    D ○ All thirty one-people looked bored.

25. **A** ○ We like to visit the wonderful muse-ums in Chicago, Illinois.

    B ○ There are twenty seven-people in my pottery class.

    C ○ My grand-mother is ninety two years old.

    D ○ James made a pineapple upside down-cake.

Choose the sentence in which underlining is used correctly.

26. **A** ○ <u>Entertainment</u> Weekly is fun to read.

    B ○ She is the author of The <u>Way It Was Then</u>.

    C ○ "<u>Por favor</u>," said Enrique.

    D ○ <u>Gone</u> With the Wind is her favorite movie.

27. **A** ○ I saw the play Jane <u>Eyre</u> four times.

    B ○ Do you read the <u>Wall Street Journal</u>?

    C ○ I checked that fact in <u>World Book</u> Encyclopedia.

    D ○ Have you read the book Huckleberry <u>Finn</u>?

Name _____   Date _____

Writing Sentences

> - Every sentence has a base consisting of a simple subject and a simple predicate.
>   EXAMPLE: People applied.
> - Expand the meaning of a sentence by adding adjectives, adverbs, and prepositional phrases to the sentence base.
>   EXAMPLE: **Several** people applied **at the technical institute last week.**

A. Expand the meaning of each sentence base below by adding adjectives, adverbs, and prepositional phrases. Write your expanded sentence.

1. (Visitors toured.) _____

2. (Machines roared.) _____

3. (People lifted.) _____

4. (Work stopped.) _____

5. (Buzzer sounded.) _____

B. Imagine two different scenes for each sentence base below. Write an expanded sentence to describe each scene you imagine.

1. (Day began.) **a.** _____

   b. _____

2. (Workers operated.) **a.** _____

   b. _____

3. (Supervisor explained.) **a.** _____

   b. _____

4. (Shipment arrived.) **a.** _____

   b. _____

5. (People unpacked.) **a.** _____

   b. _____

6. (Automobiles appeared.) **a.** _____

   b. _____

7. (Friend cooked.) **a.** _____

   b. _____

Writing Paragraphs

> ■ A **paragraph** is a group of sentences about one **main idea.** All the sentences in a paragraph relate to the main idea.
> ■ The first sentence in a paragraph is always indented.
>   EXAMPLE:
>   People work for a variety of reasons. One of the most important reasons people work is to earn money to buy goods and services they need. Work can also provide enjoyment or lead to achieving personal goals.

A. In each paragraph below, cross out the sentence that is not related to the main idea of the paragraph. Then write a new sentence that is related.

1.   Bob and Todd have been friends since the day Bob's family first moved into the neighborhood. The boys were in the same class in both kindergarten and first grade. A few years later, they joined Scouts and worked together to earn merit badges. Bob's dad is an experienced carpenter. In junior high school, Bob was a star pitcher, while Todd led their team in batting.

_____

2.   Rita's first job was at the swimming pool. Because she was a good swimmer and had passed a lifesaving course, she was asked to demonstrate swimming strokes during swimming instruction. She was not old enough to be an instructor. Sometimes she got jobs baby-sitting for families with children in the swimming program.

_____

B. Choose one of the topics below, and write a paragraph of three or four sentences that are related to it.

a. Your first job	**c.** The job you'd most like to have
b. The job everyone wants	**d.** Jobs in your community

_____

_____

_____

_____

_____

_____

_____

_____

_____

Writing Topic Sentences

> ■ The **topic sentence** states the main idea of a paragraph. It is often placed at the beginning of a paragraph.
>   EXAMPLE:
>   Young people can learn various skills by working in a fast-food restaurant. They can learn how to use machines to cook food in a uniform way, how to handle money, and how to work with customers and with other employees.

A. Underline the topic sentence in each paragraph below.

1. Working in a fast-food restaurant is a good first job for young people. The hours are flexible. No previous experience is needed. The work is not hard.

2. A popular ice cream parlor in our town hires young people. Some work serving customers. Some work making special desserts. Others do cleanup and light maintenance.

3. Computers are used in fast-food restaurants. The cash register has a computer that totals purchase prices and computes change. Ovens and deep fryers have computers that regulate cooking temperatures.

B. Write a topic sentence for each group of related sentences.

1. Working may conflict with other activities. There may not be enough time for you to complete housework. You may miss out on having fun with friends.

    Topic Sentence: _____

2. Kate manages the kitchen, plans the menus, and orders all the food. Jesse supervises the dining room. Jesse's sister does the bookkeeping for the restaurant. On weekends, my brother and I help clear the tables.

    Topic Sentence: _____

3. The dining room was decorated with advertisements from the Fifties. The band played only music from the Fifties, and the waiters and waitresses all wore black slacks and bright pink bow ties.

    Topic Sentence: _____

C. Write a topic sentence for one of the topics below.

        a. The best restaurant I've ever gone to   **c.** The job of waiter
        b. Restaurants in our town   **d.** The worst meal I've ever eaten

_____

_____

_____

Writing Supporting Details

> ■ The idea expressed in a topic sentence can be developed with sentences containing **supporting details.** Details can include facts, examples, and reasons.

A. Circle the topic sentence, and underline four supporting details in the paragraph below.

In almost every professional sport, there are far more applicants than available jobs. Consider professional football. Every season, several hundred players are selected by twenty-eight professional football teams. Of those chosen, only about ten percent are actually signed by a professional team. Furthermore, this number shrinks each year because team owners want smaller and smaller teams.

B. Answer the following questions about the supporting details you underlined.

1. What is one supporting detail that is a fact?

_____

_____

_____

_____

2. What is a supporting detail that is a reason?

_____

_____

_____

C. Read each topic sentence below, and write three supporting details for each.

1. People who want a career in sports could teach physical education.

_____

_____

_____

2. Professional sports teams employ people other than players.

_____

_____

_____

_____

Topic and Audience

> ■ The **topic** of a piece of writing is the subject written about.
> ■ The **audience** is the person or persons who will read what is written.
>   EXAMPLES: parents, teenagers, school officials, engineers

A. Choose the most likely audience for each topic listed below.

        a. parents   **c.** job counselors
        b. high-school students   **d.** computer hobbyists

_____ **1.** future of personal computers   _____ **3.** jobs of the future

_____ **2.** benefits of a college education   _____ **4.** paying for college

B. Read the paragraph below, and answer the questions that follow.

The evening was full of surprises. First, Brenda forgot to tell me she had five children. I had seen only two of them at the store with her. She also forgot to mention the cats—to which I am violently allergic. Also, I wasn't prepared to fix the children dinner. I wrongly assumed that Brenda would have fed them before I came. After getting everyone settled, I wondered if I should do the dishes. I figured that anyone with five children would appreciate having that job done.

1. What is the topic? _____

2. Name two possible audiences for the paragraph.

_____

_____

3. Explain why each audience might be interested.

_____

_____

_____

_____

C. Choose two topics that interest you. Write a topic sentence for a paragraph about each topic. Then name an audience for each paragraph.

1. Topic Sentence: _____

    Audience: _____

2. Topic Sentence: _____

    Audience: _____

Name _____   Date _____

Brainstorming

> ■ **Brainstorming** is a way to bring as many ideas to mind as you can. You can brainstorm by yourself or with others. As you brainstorm, write down your ideas. It is not necessary to write your ideas in sentence form.

A. Brainstorm about the things you would do if you were president of a major corporation. Write your ideas below.

1. _____

2. _____

3. _____

4. _____

B. Read the topics below. Choose one topic, and circle it. Then brainstorm about its advantages and disadvantages. Write down as many ideas as you can.

a. volunteering   **d.** bicycle helmet laws

b. eating healthy   **e.** automatic seat belts

c. mediating disagreements   **f.** self-defense training

1. _____

2. _____

3. _____

4. _____

5. _____

6. _____

C. Now write a brief paragraph about the topic you chose in Exercise B that explains either the advantages or disadvantages of the topic.

_____

_____

_____

_____

_____

Outlining

■ Before you write, organize your thoughts by making an **outline.** An outline consists of the title of the topic, headings for the main ideas, and subheadings for the supporting details.

■ Main headings are listed after Roman numerals. Subheadings are listed after capital letters. Details are listed after Arabic numerals.

EXAMPLE:

Topic	Should Young People Be Paid for Doing Chores?
Main heading	I. Benefits to parents
Subheadings	A. Chores get done
	B. More leisure time
Main heading	II. Benefits to young people
Subheading	A. Learn useful skills
Details	1. Clean and do laundry
	2. Budget time
Subheading	B. Become responsible

■ **Choose a topic that interests you. Then write an outline for that topic, using the example outline as a guide.**

_____

_____

_____

_____

_____

_____

_____

_____

_____

_____

_____

_____

_____

_____

_____

Name _____   Date _____

Persuasive Composition

> ■ The writer of a **persuasive composition** tries to convince others to accept a personal opinion.

A. Read the following persuasive composition.

<u>Everyone Should Learn to Use a Computer</u>

    Knowing how to use a computer is an essential skill for everyone who wants to succeed in today's world. One basic computer program that everyone should learn to use is the word processing program. Most types of writing are easily and professionally produced with a word processing program. For example, everyone must occasionally write a business letter. Using a computer allows you to arrange and rearrange information easily, making your writing more clear and accurate. Word processing programs can help you check your spelling and grammar. A computer makes it easy to correct mistakes.

    Computers can be used for much more than word processing, however. Other areas of interest and opportunity in the field of computers are graphic design, programming, and creating new games. Jobs in the computer field are growing, and strong computer skills can serve you well now and into the future.

B. Answer the questions below.

1. List three facts the writer includes to persuade the reader.

_____

_____

_____

_____

_____

2. List two reasons the writer includes in the composition.

_____

_____

_____

3. List one example the writer uses to support the topic.

_____

_____

_____

C. Choose one of the topic sentences below. Write a short paragraph in which you use facts to persuade your audience about the topic.

1. The driver and front-seat passenger in a car face various consequences if they don't wear seat belts.

2. More people should car-pool or use public transportation.

_____

_____

_____

_____

_____

_____

D. Choose one of the topic sentences below. Write a short paragraph in which you use reasons to persuade your audience about the topic.

1. Wearing seat belts ensures all passengers of a safer ride.

2. The most important subject a person can learn about is _____ .

_____

_____

_____

_____

_____

_____

E. Choose one of the topic sentences below. Write a short paragraph in which you use an example to persuade your audience about the topic.

1. I know someone who wore a seat belt and survived a serious collision.

2. _____ make the best pets.

_____

_____

_____

_____

_____

_____

Revising and Proofreading

- **Revising** gives you a chance to rethink and review what you have written and to improve your writing. Revise by adding words and information, by deleting unneeded words and information, and by moving words, sentences, and paragraphs around.
- **Proofreading** has to do with checking spelling, punctuation, grammar, and capitalization. Use proofreader's marks to show changes needed.

Proofreader's Marks

	Reverse the order.	Take something out.
Capitalize.	Add a period.	Correct spelling.
Make a small letter.	Add quotation marks.	Indent for new paragraph.
Add a comma.	Add something.	Move something.

A. Rewrite the paragraph below. Correct the errors by following the proofreader's marks.

¶ personal safety is one of the most important social issues today. Adults and children are worried about staying safe in all these places their homes, their schools, and the places they go to have fun. one of the best things a person can do is to act with confidence and awarness. Confidents means "believing" and Awareness means seeing." Several studies have shone that people who act with confidence and awareness do not look like easy targets which is what criminals look for.

_____

_____

_____

_____

_____

_____

_____

_____

_____

Name _____ Date _____

B. Read the paragraphs below. Use proofreader's marks to revise and proofread the paragraphs. Then write your revised paragraphs below.

When your outside your home, your body Language is important very. if you straigt stand, walk purposefully and pay attention to what is around you you will discourage Criminals because you appear strong and alert. along with confidence and awareness Another tool you can use all the time is your voice you can yell. Crimnals dont like to draw to attention themselves and they don't like to be seen. Yelling may sometimes be embarrassing, but your safety is more important than worrying about imbarrassment.

at home, its important to always keep your doors and windows locked you should never opent the door to someone you don't know. You don't have to be polite to somebody who may be trying to do you harm. This also applys to the telephone. If sombody you don't know calls and tries to keep you engaged in a conservation, just hang up. you don't have to be polite to somebody who is intruding in your life, especially if you don't know the person. always Keep your safety in mind and act in a way that discourages criminals from bothering you

_____
_____
_____
_____
_____
_____
_____
_____
_____
_____
_____
_____
_____
_____

Name _____   Date _____

Unit 5 Test

Read the paragraph. Then choose the correct answer to each question.

As a singles tennis player, John McEnroe has won the U.S. Open title on four occasions, and he has won the prestigious Wimbledon championship three different times. McEnroe has also won over eight major doubles tournaments since joining the professional tour in 1978. McEnroe is noted for his powerful serve-and-volley game, but it is his agility and quickness which sports fans admire most. Perhaps most important of all, McEnroe's tennis game has no weaknesses.

1. Which sentence could best be used as a topic sentence for the paragraph above?

    A ○ John McEnroe has recently attempted a comeback in tennis.

    B ○ John McEnroe has often had conflicts with officials during tennis matches.

    C ○ John McEnroe plays tennis well on all court surfaces.

    D ○ John McEnroe is one of the most talented tennis players in the world.

2. Which sentence would add the most appropriate supporting detail to the paragraph above?

    A ○ McEnroe has a single-minded approach, which helps make him a champion.

    B ○ McEnroe was born in Wiesbaden, West Germany.

    C ○ McEnroe will be thirty-five years old soon.

    D ○ One of McEnroe's doubles partners was Peter Fleming.

3. Which audience would be the most interested in this paragraph?

    A ○ preschoolers   **B** ○ bus drivers   **C** ○ grandparents   **D** ○ athletes

4. What does the author use most to persuade readers to accept his or her opinion about John McEnroe?

    A ○ examples   **B** ○ facts   **C** ○ reasons

Choose the correct answer to each question.

5. Which would you use to bring as many ideas to mind as possible?

    A ○ outlining   **B** ○ brainstorming   **C** ○ persuading

6. Which would be an example of persuasive writing?

    A ○ letter to the editor   **B** ○ report   **C** ○ outline

7. What is the subject of a piece of writing called?

    A ○ example   **B** ○ detail   **C** ○ topic

8. Which is a group of sentences about one main idea?

    A ○ topic sentences   **B** ○ outline   **C** ○ paragraph

9. Which is not included in supporting details about a topic?

    A ○ outlines   **B** ○ facts   **C** ○ reasons

10. Which states the main idea of a paragraph?

    A ○ example   **B** ○ topic sentence   **C** ○ reason

Name _____   Date _____

Use the outline to answer the questions.

Topic: Staying Fit and Healthy
  I. Food
    A. Eating right
    B. _____
      1. Vitamins
      2. Minerals
  II. _____
    A. Walking
    B. Running
    C. Other
      1. Weights
      2. Machines
  III. _____
    A. Mind/body
    B. Positive thinking

11. Which best fits in the blank for II.?

A ○ Attitude

B ○ Exercise

C ○ Weights

12. Which best fits in the blank for I. B.?

A ○ Exercise

B ○ Essential nutrients

C ○ Attitude

13. Which best fits in the blank for III.?

A ○ Attitude

B ○ Weights

C ○ Exercise

Choose the sentence that shows correct use of proofreader's marks for the underlined sentence.

14. barb ted chris and I went kamping in august

A ○ barb ted chris and i went kamping in august

B ○ barb ted chris and i went kamping in august

C ○ barb ted chris and i went kamping in august

15. since i first was in line i bought the tikets

A ○ since i first was in line i bought the tikets

B ○ since i first was in line i bought the tikets

C ○ since i first was in line i bought the tikets

Choose the sentence that is the correct revision of the underlined sentence.

16. I although understood what the spanish speaker was saying Ms. Cartim did not.

A ○ I understood what the speaker was saying, Ms. Carlim did not.

B ○ I although understood what the Spanish speaker was saying, Ms. Carlim did not.

C ○ Although I understood what the speaker was saying, Ms. Carlim did not.

17. dont let me foget to stop by at the post office and mail this letter

A ○ Don't let me forget to stop at the office and post mail this letter

B ○ Please don't let me forget to stop at the post office and mail this letter.

C ○ Please don't let me stop by the post office and mail this letter.

Name _____   Date _____

Dictionary: Syllables

- A **syllable** is a part of a word that is pronounced at one time. Dictionary entry words are divided into syllables to show how they can be divided at the end of a writing line.
- A **hyphen** (-) is placed between syllables to separate them.
  EXAMPLE: neigh-bor-hood
- If a word has a beginning or ending syllable of only one letter, do not divide it so that one letter stands alone.
  EXAMPLES: a-bout   bur-y

A. Find each word in a dictionary. Then write each word with a hyphen between each syllable.

1. rummage _____

2. nevertheless _____

3. abominable _____

4. silhouette _____

5. biological _____

6. stationery _____

7. correspondence _____

8. character _____

9. enthusiasm _____

10. abandon _____

11. treacherous _____

12. effortless _____

13. romantic _____

14. nautical _____

15. accelerate _____

16. financial _____

17. significance _____

18. unimportant _____

19. commercial _____

20. ballerina _____

B. Write two ways in which each word may be divided at the end of a writing line.

1. imagination _____imag-ination_____   _____imagina-tion_____

2. unexplainable _____   _____

3. tropical _____   _____

4. accomplishment _____   _____

5. encyclopedia _____   _____

6. librarian _____   _____

7. astronomic _____   _____

8. efficient _____   _____

9. cleanliness _____   _____

Name _____   Date _____

Dictionary: Definitions and Parts of Speech

- A dictionary lists the **definitions** of each entry word. Many words have more than one definition. In this case, the most commonly used definition is given first. Sometimes a definition is followed by a sentence showing a use of the entry word.
- A dictionary also tells the **part of speech** for each entry word. An abbreviation (shown below) stands for each part of speech. Some words may be used as more than one part of speech.
    EXAMPLE: **need** (nēd) *n.* **1.** the lack of something wanted or necessary. **2.** something wanted or necessary: *What are your basic needs for the camping trip?* -*v.* to require.

- **Use the dictionary samples below to answer the questions.**

pop-u-lar (pop′ yə lər) *adj.* **1.** pleasing to many people. **2.** having many friends: *Angela was voted the most popular girl in her class.* **3.** accepted by the general public: *The idea that pencils contain lead is a popular error.*
por-poise (pôr′ pəs) *n.* a warm-blooded marine mammal that is related to the dolphin.

por-tion (pôr′ shən) *n.* **1.** a part of a whole: *We spent a portion of the day at the park.* **2.** a part or share of a whole belonging to a person or a group. **3.** a helping of food served to one person. -*v.* to divide into parts or shares.
por-tray (pôr trā′) *v.* **1.** to draw or paint a picture of: *The artist portrayed the beautiful mountains in a painting.* **2.** to give a picture of in words; describe.

1. Which word can be used as either a noun

   or a verb? _____

2. Which entry word has the most example

   sentences? _____

n.	noun
pron.	pronoun
v.	verb
adj.	adjective
adv.	adverb
prep.	preposition

3. What part of speech is porpoise?

   _____

4. How many definitions are given for the word porpoise? _____

   for portion? _____   for portray? _____

5. Write the most commonly used definition of popular. _____

   _____

6. Use the first definition of popular in a sentence. _____

   _____

7. Write a sentence in which you use portion as a verb. _____

   _____

8. Use the second definition of portray in a sentence. _____

   _____

Dictionary: Etymologies

- Many dictionary entries include an **etymology** which is the origin and development of a word.
- An etymology is usually enclosed in brackets [ ] after the definition of the entry word. The symbol < stands for the phrase "is derived from" or "comes from."
  - EXAMPLE: **razor** [Middle English *rasor* < Old French *raser,* to scrape.]
  - The word <u>razor</u> came into English from the Middle English word <u>rasor</u>, which came from the Old French word <u>raser</u>, which meant "to scrape."

■ **Use the dictionary entries below to answer the questions.**

nov-el (nov´əl) *n.* a long piece of prose fiction with a detailed plot. *-adj.* new, strange, unusual. [Old French *novelle,* unique, from Latin *novella,* new things.]

pueb-lo (pweb´lō) *n.* **1.** a Native American dwelling made of adobe and stone which houses many people. **2. Pueblo.** a member of a Native American tribe that lives in pueblos. [Spanish *pueblo,* people or village, from Latin *populus,* people.]

punk (pungk) *n.* **1.** a dry, light, brownish substance that burns very slowly, often used to light fireworks. **2.** dry, decayed wood, used in its dry state as tinder. [Probably from Algonquin *punk,* live ashes.]

reef (rēf) *n.* part of a sail that can be rolled or folded up to reduce the amount of the sail exposed to the wind. *-v.* to roll or fold up a part of a sail. [Old Norse *rifridge.*]

1. Which word probably came from the Algonquin language? _____

2. Which languages are in the history of the word <u>novel</u>?

_____

3. Which word originally meant "live ashes"? _____

4. Which word comes from the word <u>populus</u>? _____

5. Which words have more than one language in their history? _____

_____

6. What is the meaning of the Latin word <u>novella</u>? _____

7. Which word is spelled the same in English as it is in Spanish?

_____

8. From what language did the Old French word <u>novelle</u> come?

_____

9. Which words came into English from only one earlier language? _____

_____

10. Which word comes from a word that meant "people"? _____

11. Which word comes from the word <u>rifridge</u>? _____

Using Parts of a Book

- A **title page** tells the name of a book and its author.
- A **copyright page** tells who published the book, where it was published, and when it was published.
- A **table of contents** lists the chapter or unit titles and the page numbers on which they begin. It is at the front of a book.
- An **index** gives a detailed list of the topics in a book and the page numbers on which each topic is found. It is in the back of a book.

A. Answer the questions below.

1. Where would you look to find the name of a book's author?

_____

2. Where would you look if you wanted to know how many chapters were in a book?

_____

3. Where would you find the year in which a book was published?

_____

4. Where would you find the page number on which a particular topic is found?

_____

B. Use the table of contents below to answer the questions.

1. What is this book about? _____

2. On what pages can you read about amphibians? _____

3. On what pages can you read about why venoms work? _____

4. What can you read about on pages 24–25? _____

5. What can you read about on pages 38–39? _____

6. Does the book contain a glossary? _____

Using the Library

- Books are arranged on library shelves according to **call numbers**. Each book is assigned a number from 000 to 999, according to its subject matter. The following are the main subject groups for call numbers:

000–099 Reference	500–599 Science and Mathematics
100–199 Philosophy	600–699 Technology
200–299 Religion	700–799 The Arts
300–399 Social Sciences	800–899 Literature
400–499 Languages	900–999 History and Geography

A. Write the call number group in which you would find each book.

1. *Australia: The Island Continent* _____

2. *Technology in a New Age* _____

3. *French: A Romance Language* _____

4. *Solving Word Problems in Mathematics* _____

5. *Ancient Philosophy* _____

6. *World Almanac and Book of Facts* _____

7. *Artists of the 1920's* _____

8. *Funny Poems for a Rainy Day* _____

9. *Science Experiments for Teen-agers* _____

10. *People in Society* _____

11. *Russian Folktales* _____

12. *Religions Around the World* _____

13. *World War I: The Complete Story* _____

14. *Encyclopaedia Britannica* _____

15. *The Social Characteristics of Pack Animals* _____

B. Write the titles of three of your favorite books. Write the call number range beside each title.

1. _____

2. _____

3. _____

Using the Card Catalog

- The **card catalog** contains information cards on every book in the library. Some libraries are now computerized and have no card catalogs, but the information in the computer is filed in the same manner as the information in the card catalog.
- Each book has three cards in the catalog. They are filed separately according to:
  1. the author's last name
  2. the subject of the book
  3. the title of the book

A. Use the sample catalog card to answer the questions below.

Author Card

Call number —— 331.20 Le | Leventhal, Robert —— Author
Title —— A Great Place to Visit
Place published —— —New York: | Phantom House Inc. —— Publisher
Date published —— © 1993
Number of pages —— 312 p.

1. Who is the author? _____

2. Are there any pictures or drawings in the book? _____

3. What is the book's call number? _____

4. When was the book published? _____

5. List one subject under which the subject card for this book might be filed. _____

6. Write what the heading would be for this book's title card. _____

B. Write author, title, or subject to tell which card you would look for to locate the book or books.

1. books about sports in Russia _____

2. a novel by Mark Twain _____

3. *The Invisible Man* _____

4. books about Amelia Earhart _____

5. a book of poems by Emily Dickinson _____

6. *It's a Dog's Life* _____

Using an Encyclopedia

- An **encyclopedia** is a reference book that contains articles on many different topics. The articles are arranged alphabetically in volumes. Each volume is marked to indicate which articles are inside.
- **Guide words** are used to show the first topic on each page.
- At the end of most articles there is a listing of **cross-references** that suggests related topics for the reader to investigate.
- Most encyclopedias also have an index of subject titles.

A. Find the entry for <u>Louisa May Alcott</u> in an encyclopedia. Then answer the following questions.

1. What encyclopedia did you use? _____

2. When did Louisa May Alcott live? _____

3. Where was she born? _____

4. What is the name of one of her books? _____

5. What did she do as a volunteer during the American Civil War? _____

B. Find the entry for <u>Medic Alert</u> in an encyclopedia. Then answer the questions.

1. What encyclopedia did you use? _____

2. The Medic Alert emblem can be worn as a _____ .

3. What organization provides the Medic Alert emblems? _____

4. What kind of information does the emblem give about the person wearing it?

   _____

5. Whose telephone number appears on the emblem? _____

C. Find the entry in an encyclopedia for a person in whom you are interested. Then answer the following questions.

1. Who is your subject? _____

2. What encyclopedia did you use? _____

3. When did the person live? _____

4. What is it about the person that makes him or her famous? _____

   _____

5. What cross-references are listed? _____

Name _____   Date _____

Using an Encyclopedia Index

> - Most encyclopedias have an **index** of subject titles, listed in alphabetical order.
> - The index shows the volume and the page number where an article is found.
> - Some encyclopedias contain articles on many different topics. Some encyclopedias contain many different articles relating to a broad general topic.

- **Use the sample encyclopedia index entry to answer the questions.**

Index

Alligator, 1–6; 11–389; *see* Crocodile; Reptile
Bear, 1–35
   Black, 1–37
   Brown, 1–36
   Grizzly, 1–37
   Polar, 1–39
Cougar, 2–53; *see* Bobcat; Mountain Lion
Crocodile, 2–79; 11–389 *see* Alligator; Reptile
Dingo, 3–94

---

1. In what volume would you find an article on grizzly bears? _____

2. On what pages would you find information on crocodiles? _____

3. Are all articles on bears found in the same volume? _____

4. On page 6 you would find an article about what animal? _____

5. What are the cross-references for **Alligator**? _____

6. Do the words in bold show the name of the volume or the name of the animal? _____

7. Which animals have articles in two volumes? _____

8. In which volume would you expect to find information on reptiles? _____

9. Information on what animal is found in Volume 3? _____

10. If you looked under **Bobcat**, what might you expect to find as cross-references? _____

11. Information on what animal is found on page 79 in the encyclopedia? _____

12. Which of the following would be the most likely title of this encyclopedia? _____

   a. Encyclopedia of Reptiles   **b.** Encyclopedia of Mammals   **c.** Encyclopedia of Wild Animals

---

Using a Thesaurus

> ■ A **thesaurus** is a reference book that writers use to find the exact words they need. Like a dictionary, a thesaurus lists its entry words alphabetically. Each entry word has a list of **synonyms,** or words that can be used in its place. Some thesauruses also list **antonyms** for the entry word.
>
> EXAMPLE: You have just written the following sentence:
> The children **laughed** as the tiny puppy licked their faces.
> With the help of a thesaurus, you could improve the sentence by replacing laughed with its more precise synonym giggled.
> The children **giggled** as the tiny puppy licked their faces.

A. Use the thesaurus sample below to answer the questions.

> **move** *v. syn.* turn, budge, shift, retrieve, carry, transport, retreat, crawl, arouse, progress. *ant.* stay, stop, stabilize

1. Which is the entry word? _____

2. What are its synonyms? _____

   _____

3. Which word would you use in place of excite? _____

4. Which word would you use in place of rotate? _____

5. What are the antonyms of move? _____

6. Which antonym would you use in place of remain? _____

B. Use the synonyms of <u>move</u> to complete the sentences.

1. Sharon asked me if I would _____ the groceries in from the car.

2. Spot was able to _____ the golf ball from the lake.

3. Ryan's job is to _____ fruit from Michigan to other parts of the country.

4. The surfer had to _____ his weight from one leg to the other to keep his balance.

5. The instructor asked the students to _____ around in their chairs so they could see the map.

6. A baby has to _____ in order to get around.

7. We hope to _____ steadily up the mountain by climbing from ledge to ledge.

8. Robert wouldn't _____ from his favorite spot under the kitchen table.

Name _____   Date _____

Using the *Readers' Guide*

> ■ The ***Readers' Guide to Periodical Literature*** lists by author and by
> subject all the articles that appear in nearly two hundred magazines.
> Use the *Readers' Guide* when you need
> ● recent articles on a particular subject,
> ● several articles written over a period of time about the same subject,
> ● many articles written by the same author.

■ **Use the *Readers' Guide* samples to answer the questions below.**

Subject Entry

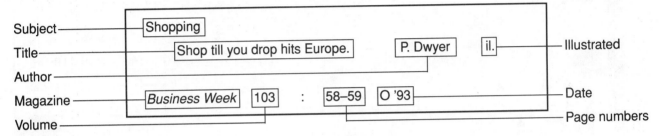

Author Entry

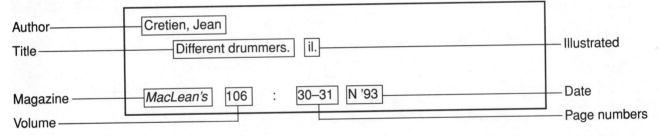

1. Who wrote the article "Shop Till You Drop Hits Europe"? _____

2. Who is the author of "Different Drummers"? _____

3. In what magazine will you find the article "Shop Till You Drop Hits Europe"? _____

4. Under what subject entry can you find the article "Shop Till You Drop Hits Europe"? _____

5. In what volume of *MacLean's* does "Different Drummers" appear? _____

6. In what month and year was "Different Drummers" published? _____

7. Which article is illustrated? _____

8. In what month and year was "Shop Till You Drop Hits Europe" published? _____

9. On what pages will you find "Different Drummers"? _____

10. On what pages will you find the article "Shop Till You Drop Hits Europe"? _____

Name _____   Date _____

Using an Atlas

> ■ An **atlas** is a reference book that uses maps to organize pertinent facts
> about states, provinces, countries, continents, and bodies of water.
> Additional maps show information on topography; resources, industry, and
> agriculture; vegetation; population; and climate.

A. Use the sample atlas entry to answer the questions below.

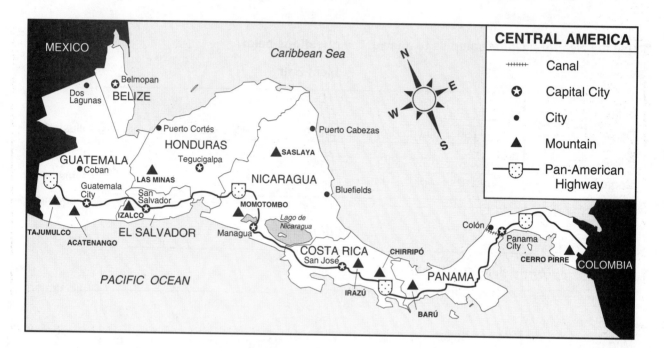

1. What part of the world is shown on this map? _____

2. How many countries make up Central America? _____

3. Which mountain is farthest west? _____

4. What major highway is shown on the map? _____

5. Which country has no mountains? _____

6. What is the capital of Nicaragua? _____

B. Answer the questions.

1. What kind of map would you use to find out where most mining occurs in a country? _____

2. Would a topographical map show you where the most people live or where the most mountains are? _____

_____

3. What kind of map would you use to decide what clothes to pack for a July trip to Japan? _____

Name _____   Date _____

Using an Almanac

> ■ An **almanac** is a reference book that presents useful information on a wide variety of topics. Much of this information is in the form of tables, charts, graphs, and time lines.

■ **Use the sample almanac page to answer the questions.**

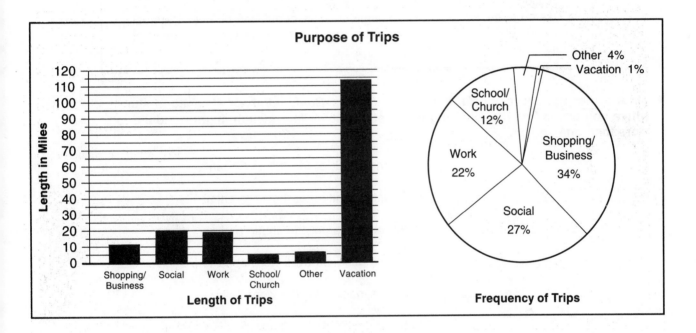

1. Which trip accounts for the most miles traveled? _____

2. What reason do most people give for taking trips? _____

3. Which three purposes together account for 60% of all trips? _____

4. Which graph shows how often people travel for a specific purpose? _____

5. Which trips are the shortest? _____

6. Do people travel farther for work or for social reasons? _____

7. Out of 100 trips, how many are made for shopping/business reasons? _____

8. What is the length of the trip least often taken? _____

9. What is the length of the trip most often taken? _____

10. Do people travel more often for school/church or for social reasons? _____

Choosing Reference Sources

- Use a **dictionary** to find definitions of words, pronunciations of words, word usage suggestions, and etymologies, or word histories.
- Use an **encyclopedia** to find articles about many different people and things. Also use an encyclopedia to find references to related subjects.
- Use a **thesaurus** to find synonyms and antonyms.
- Use the *Readers' Guide to Periodical Literature* to find magazine articles on specific subjects or by particular authors.
- Use an **atlas** to find maps and other information about geographical locations.
- Use an **almanac** to find information such as population numbers, annual rainfall, election statistics, and other specific information over a period of one year.

■ Write <u>dictionary</u>, <u>encyclopedia</u>, <u>thesaurus</u>, *Readers' Guide*, <u>atlas</u>, or <u>almanac</u> to show where you would find the following information. Some information might be found in more than one source.

_____ 1. the depth of the Indian Ocean

_____ 2. the definition of the word <u>animosity</u>

_____ 3. an article on parachuting

_____ 4. the usages of the word <u>speckle</u>

_____ 5. a synonym for the word <u>build</u>

_____ 6. an article on the latest development in cancer research

_____ 7. the pronunciation of the word <u>pneumonia</u>

_____ 8. the largest lake in Louisiana

_____ 9. facts about the life of Abraham Lincoln

_____ 10. a synonym for the word <u>begin</u>

_____ 11. information about John F. Kennedy's presidency

_____ 12. the origin of the word <u>immortal</u>

_____ 13. recent articles on home fire prevention

_____ 14. the history of the French Revolution

_____ 15. the average January temperature in Santa Fe, New Mexico

_____ 16. the states through which the Mississippi River runs

_____ 17. an antonym for the word <u>answer</u>

Name _____   Date _____

Using Reference Sources

> ■ Use reference sources—dictionaries, encyclopedias, the *Readers' Guide to Periodical Literature,* thesauruses, atlases, and almanacs—to find information about people, places, or things with which you are not familiar. You can also use these sources to learn more about subjects that interest you.

A. Follow the directions below.

1. Find the entry for your state in one of the reference sources. Write the exact title

   of the reference source. _____

2. Write a brief summary of the information you found about your state.

   _____

   _____

   _____

   _____

   _____

   _____

B. Follow the directions, and answer the questions.

1. Choose a famous person you would like to know more about.

   Person's name: _____

2. List two reference sources you can use to find information about this person.

   1. _____   2. _____

3. Use one of the sources you listed above to find out when the person was born.

   Write the date of birth. _____

4. Use the appropriate reference source to find the title of the most recent article written about the person. Write the title of the article.

   _____

5. Use either reference source you listed in number two. Find the entry for the person you are researching. Write a short summary of the information you found.

   _____

   _____

   _____

Name _____ Date _____

C. Follow the directions, and answer the questions.

1. Choose a country you would like to learn more about.

   Name of country: _____

2. List four reference sources you can use to find information about this country.

   1. _____   3. _____

   2. _____   4. _____

3. Use one reference source to find the title of the most recent article written about the country. Write the title of the article.

   _____

4. Use one reference source to find out the capital of the country. Write the name

   of the capital. _____

5. Use another reference source to find out on what continent the country is located.

   Write the name of the continent. _____

6. Find the entry for the country in any one of the reference sources you listed in number two. Write the exact title of the reference source.

   _____

7. Write a short summary of the information you found. Do not include information given in number 3, 4, or 5.

   _____

   _____

   _____

   _____

   _____

8. Find the entry for the country in one other reference source. Write

   the exact title of the reference source. _____

9. What new information did you learn about the country?

   _____

   _____

   _____

Name _____   Date _____

Unit 6 Test

Refer to the dictionary samples to answer the questions that follow.

plunge (plunj) *v.* **1.** to throw oneself, as into water: *I plunged into the cool lake.* **2.** to enter suddenly into some condition: *The two sides plunged into war. -n.* the act of plunging; a dive. [Middle English *plungen*, from Old French, from Latin *plumbum*, to lead.]

pow-der (pou´der) *n.* **1.** a dry substance of fine particles produced by crushing, grinding, etc. **2.** a specific kind of powder:

I cleaned the soap powder from the washing machine. -v. **1.** to cover with powder: *The chef powdered the rolling pin.* **2.** to make into powder. [Middle English, from Old French, from Latin *pulveris*, dust.]

prairie (prâr´ē) *n.* **1.** An extensive area of flat or rolling grassland, especially the plains of central North America. [Old French *praerie*, from Latin *pratum*, meadow.]

1. Which word has one syllable?

   A ○ plunge   **B** ○ powder   **C** ○ prairie

2. Which word originally meant "dust"?

   A ○ plunge   **B** ○ powder   **C** ○ prairie

3. Which word serves as only one part of speech?

   A ○ plunge   **B** ○ powder   **C** ○ prairie

4. Which word has the most definitions?

   A ○ plunge   **B** ○ powder   **C** ○ prairie

5. Which word comes from two other languages?

   A ○ plunge   **B** ○ powder   **C** ○ prairie

6. Which word is not used in an example?

   A ○ plunge   **B** ○ powder   **C** ○ prairie

7. What does <u>plumbum</u> mean?

   A ○ dust   **B** ○ to lead   **C** ○ meadow

8. From how many other languages does <u>powder</u> come?

   A ○ two   **B** ○ three   **C** ○ four

Tell which reference source you would use to find the following information. Choose (A) for encyclopedia, (B) for dictionary, (C) for *Readers' Guide*, or (D) for atlas.

9. the usages of the word <u>spectacular</u>   **A** ○   **B** ○   **C** ○   **D** ○

10. information about glass manufacturing   **A** ○   **B** ○   **C** ○   **D** ○

11. an article written by Stella Stephens   **A** ○   **B** ○   **C** ○   **D** ○

12. the distance from Atlanta to Savannah, Georgia   **A** ○   **B** ○   **C** ○   **D** ○

13. a recent article on medical breakthroughs   **A** ○   **B** ○   **C** ○   **D** ○

14. the elevation of Mount Everest   **A** ○   **B** ○   **C** ○   **D** ○

Tell which kind of catalog card you would refer to in order to find the book(s). Choose (A) for author card, (B) for subject card, or (C) for title card.

15. *Romeo and Juliet*   **A** ○   **B** ○   **C** ○

16. a book by Jessica Sain   **A** ○   **B** ○   **C** ○

17. books about the civil rights movement   **A** ○   **B** ○   **C** ○

18. a book of poems by George Ailworth   **A** ○   **B** ○   **C** ○

19. *Moby Dick*   **A** ○   **B** ○   **C** ○

Name _____   Date _____

Choose the correct syllable division for the underlined word.

20. <u>counselor</u>

A ○ coun-se-lor

B ○ couns-e-lor

C ○ co-un-se-lor

D ○ coun-sel-or

21. <u>pantomime</u>

A ○ pan-to-mime

B ○ pant-o-mime

C ○ pan-tom-ime

D ○ pant-om-ime

Choose the item that matches the definition.

22. origin and development of a word

A ○ definition

B ○ part of speech

C ○ etymology

D ○ cross-reference

23. listing of related topics

A ○ guide words

B ○ cross-reference

C ○ part of speech

D ○ etymology

Choose the part of a book where the information can be found.

24. the book's author

A ○ title page

B ○ copyright page

C ○ table of contents

D ○ index

26. the number of chapters

A ○ title page

B ○ copyright page

C ○ table of contents

D ○ index

25. the page number for a topic

A ○ title page

B ○ copyright page

C ○ table of contents

D ○ index

27. the year the book was published

A ○ title page

B ○ copyright page

C ○ table of contents

D ○ index

Choose the item that matches the definition.

28. contains articles on many different topics

A ○ dictionary

B ○ encyclopedia

C ○ *Readers' Guide*

D ○ thesaurus

30. used to find word usage and etymologies

A ○ dictionary

B ○ *Readers' Guide*

C ○ thesaurus

D ○ encyclopedia

29. lists by author and subject all articles in many magazines

A ○ almanac

B ○ *Readers' Guide*

C ○ encyclopedia

D ○ atlas

31. presents specific information over a period of one year

A ○ almanac

B ○ atlas

C ○ encyclopedia

D ○ dictionary

Answer Key

Assessment Test (Pages 8–11)

A. 1. H **2.** S **3.** A **4.** S **B. 1.** inch **C. 1.** S **2.** C **3.** P **4.** P **D. 1.** they have **2.** we will **E.** generous **F. 1.** a **G.** The words in bold should be circled. **1.** E; (You), **Look 2.** IM; (You), **hand 3.** IN; you, **are 4.** D; I, **leave H. 1.** CS **2.** CP **I. 1.** RO **2.** CS **3.** I **J.** The word "prescription" should be labeled DO. <u>The doctor handed Jesse the prescription</u> [that he needed]. In exercises K–S, the words in bold should be circled. **K. Ms. Chang,** <u>group</u>, <u>tour</u>, **Jefferson Memorial L.** <u>uncle</u>, **Tom Fiske**, **M. 1.** past **2.** future **3.** present **4.** future **N. 1.** are, go **2.** sat, laid **3.** learn, take **4.** Set, sitting **O.** <u>2</u> should be circled. **P. 1.** IP; **Nobody 2.** OP; **him 3.** PP; **its 4.** SP; **He Q. Janet and Jason,** their **R. 1.** adjective **2.** adverb **3.** adjective **4.** adjective **5.** adjective **6.** adverb **S.** or, **about** the complaints **of** those people **T.**

591 W. Franklin Place
Bent Tree, TX 78709
Jan. 27, 19___

Dear Ms. Coleman,
  Please know that I called you at exactly 9:15, but nobody answered the phone. I hope that you'll allow me another opportunity to tell you about my work. I have exciting news! I won the national photo contest, and my picture will be in the next issue of Parks of the World.
  I look forward to speaking with you. Please call anytime this week between 10:00 and 2:30. I'll be in one of these places: my home, my office, or my car; you have all three numbers.

Sincerely,
Eric Flannery

U. 1. 3 **2.** 1 **3.** 2 **4.** 4 **V. 1.** outlining **2.** persuading **3.** brainstorming **W.** As the movie began, the crowd grew silent and concentrated on the action. **X. 1.** noun **2.** before **3.** Old French **4.** hon-or **Y. 1.** g **2.** e **3.** a **4.** d **5.** f **6.** c **7.** b **Z. 1.** The history of Western painting: a young person's guide **2.** Juliet Heslewood **3.** yes **4.** 759 HES **5.** 1996 **6.** Raintree/Steck-Vaughn **7.** 64

Unit 1: Vocabulary

Synonyms and Antonyms (P. 13)
A.–C. Answers will vary. **D. 1.** success **2.** friendly **3.** courageous **4.** unreliable **5.** specific

Homonyms (P. 14)
A. 1. weight **2.** sail **3.** browse **4.** days, inn **5.** floe **6.** boulder **7.** pier **8.** loan **9.** mist **10.** see **11.** threw, through **12.** buy, beach **13.** aisle **14.** principal **15.** meets **16.** rein **17.** brake **18.** There **19.** flew, straight **20.** allowed **B. 1.** way **2.** steel **3.** sale **4.** fair **5.** made **6.** dear **7.** eight **8.** vane or vein **9.** straight **10.** through **11.** sore **12.** board **13.** sea **14.** scent or cent **15.** pear or pair **16.** piece **17.** son **18.** blew

Homographs (P. 15)
A. 1. bear **2.** jumper **3.** saw **4.** punch **5.** mum **6.** jar **7.** ball **8.** pupil **B. 1.** saw **2.** ball **3.** jumper **4.** saw **5.** mum **6.** punch **7.** jar **8.** pupil **9.** bear **10.** ball

Prefixes (P. 16)
A. 1. rewrite **2.** displeased **3.** forewarned **4.** impossible **5.** uncertain **6.** misspell **7.** impatient **B.** Answers will vary.

Suffixes (P. 17)
A. 1. painter **2.** tireless **3.** lifelike or lifeless **4.** artist **5.** remarkable **6.** encouragement **7.** fascination **8.** childhood **9.** famous **B. 1.** reliable **2.** glorious **3.** colorless or colorful or colorist **4.** occasional **5.** fateful or fatal **6.** comfortable or comforter or comfortless **7.** hopeless or hopeful **8.** believable or believer

Contractions (P. 18)
A. Sentences will vary. **B. 1.** won't; will not **2.** Let's; Let us **3.** that's; that is **4.** don't; do not **5.** we'd; we had **6.** can't; cannot **7.** It's; It is **8.** you're; you are **9.** We'll; We will or we shall **10.** doesn't; does not

Compound Words (P. 19)
A. Students should list any twelve of the following words: sandpaper, watercolor, homemade, comeback, fallout, outcome, waterfall, homeroom, outfield, backwater, backfield, roommate, paperback, playroom, underwater, playmate, understand, playback **B.** Answers will vary.

Connotation/Denotation (P. 20)
A. 1. − ; **2.** + ; − **3.** − ; + **4.** + ; − **5.** + ; + **6.** + ; N **7.** N ; + **8.** + ; − **9.** N ; + **10.** − ; + **11.** − ; N **12.** − ; + **B.** Paragraphs will vary.

Idioms (P. 21)
A. 1. J **2.** C **3.** A or D **4.** B **5.** K **6.** F **7.** D or A **8.** H **9.** E; G **10.** I **B.** Meanings will vary.

Unit 1 TEST (Pages 22–23)
1. A **2.** C **3.** B **4.** D **5.** C **6.** A **7.** B **8.** C **9.** B **10.** A **11.** D **12.** B **13.** A **14.** C **15.** C **16.** C **17.** A **18.** B **19.** C **20.** A **21.** A **22.** B **23.** C **24.** B **25.** B **26.** B **27.** A **28.** D **29.** B **30.** C **31.** B **32.** A **33.** C **34.** A **35.** B **36.** C

Unit 2: Sentences

Recognizing Sentences (P. 24)
S should precede the following sentences, and each should end with a period: 2, 5, 6, 7, 9, 11, 12, 14, 17, 18, 19, 20, 22, 23, 26, 27, 30.

Types of Sentences (P. 25)
1. IN; ? **2.** IN; ? **3.** IM; . **4.** D; . **5.** E; ! **6.** IN; ? **7.** IM; . **8.** D; . **9.** E; ! **10.** IM; . **11.** D; . **12.** D; . or E; ! **13.** IN; ? **14.** IN; ? **15.** IM; . **16.** D; . **17.** IM; . **18.** D; . **19.** IN; ? **20.** D; . **21.** IM; . **22.** IN; ? **23.** D; . **24.** IM; . or E; ! **25.** IN; ?

Complete Subjects and Predicates (P. 26)
1. earthquake/formed **2.** oceans/are **3.** seasons/are **4.** people/waited **5.** mechanics/have **6.** line/was **7.** Iowa/was **8.** plant/is **9.** tube/was **10.** year/is **11.** Workers/discussed **12.** Fossils/show **13.** extracted,/exist **14.** Shoshone/live **15.** Georgia/built **16.** Who/originated **17.** people/watched **18.** mines/were **19.** steamboat/was **20.** Who/brought **21.** Franklin/was **22.** guests/enjoyed **23.** Academy/was **24.** visited/were **25.** Park/is **26.** States/are

Simple Subjects and Predicates (P. 27)
1. meanings for that word/<u>cover</u> **2.** oil/<u>is made</u> **3.** highway/<u>winds</u> **4.** <u>woman</u> in the black dress/<u>studied</u> **5.** <u>meadowlark</u>/<u>builds</u> **6.** making of ice cream/<u>can be</u> **7.** stories/<u>have been written</u> **8.** answer to the question/<u>was</u> **9.** sentence/<u>should begin</u> **10.** rotation of the earth on its axis/<u>causes</u> **11.** inlet of the sea between cliffs/<u>is called</u> **12.** Dutch/<u>cultivated</u> **13.** mints in the United States/<u>are located</u> **14.** *Poor Richard's Almanac*/<u>is</u> **15.** climate of Jamaica/<u>attracts</u> **16.** movie/<u>has been shown</u> **17.** Acres of wheat/<u>rippled</u> **18.** mechanic/<u>completed</u> **19.** people in that picture/<u>were boarding</u> **20.** One/<u>can find</u> **21.** city of Albuquerque, /<u>is</u> **22.** trees/<u>have</u> **23.** Sequoias, the world's tallest trees,/<u>are found</u> **24.** John Banister/<u>was</u> **25.** trees/<u>hide</u> **26.** woman/<u>filled</u>

Position of Subjects (P. 28)
1. The <u>movie</u> <u>is playing</u> when? **2.** <u>I</u> <u>will</u> never <u>forget</u> my first train trip. **3.** The <u>picture</u> I want to buy <u>is</u> here. **4.** <u>He</u> <u>has</u> seldom been ill. **5.** The <u>lights</u> <u>went</u> out. **6.** <u>Bookcases</u> <u>were</u> on all sides of the room. **7.** <u>You</u> <u>take</u> the roast from the oven. **8.** The speeding <u>car</u> <u>swerved</u> around the sharp curve. **9.** <u>You</u> <u>get</u> out of the swimming pool. **10.** <u>You</u> <u>study</u> for the spelling test. **11.** Two <u>children</u> <u>are</u> in the pool.

Compound Subjects and Predicates (P. 29)
A. 1. Lewis and Clark/blazed **2.** The rose and the jasmine/are **3.** Kelly and Amy/went **4.** Chris/<u>swept</u> the floor, <u>dusted</u> the furniture, and <u>washed</u> **5.** Empires/<u>flourish</u> and <u>decay</u>. **6.** lake/<u>rises</u> and <u>falls</u> **7.** Juanita and her brother/are **8.** <u>Dwight D. Eisenhower and Douglas MacArthur</u>/were **9.** He/<u>turned</u> slowly and then <u>answered</u> **10.** Museums, libraries, and art galleries/are **11.** The <u>typewriters</u>, the desks, and the chairs/are **12.** The plants/<u>grew</u> tall and <u>flowered</u>. **13.** Stephanie and Teresa/worked **14.** He/<u>ran</u> and <u>slid</u> **15.** clerk/<u>added</u> up the numbers and <u>wrote</u> **16.** Reading and baking/are **17.** Mary/<u>drank</u> iced tea and <u>ate</u> **18.** Cars and trucks/sped **19.** Red and blue/are **B. and C.** Sentences will vary.

Combining Sentences (P. 30) Sentences may vary.
Direct Objects (P. 31)
The words in bold should be labeled DO. **1.** prevented, **accident**.
2. should have, **appreciation 3.** pass, **potatoes 4.** Do, waste, **time**
5. did, keep, **coupons 6.** collects, **stamps 7.** invented, **gin 8.** Answer,
question 9. are picking, **trophies 10.** invented, **steamboat 11.** am
reading, *The Old Man and the Sea.* **12.** guides, **sailors 13.** gave,
alphabet 14. should study, **history 15.** made, **cake 16.** Can, find,
object 17. wrote, **story 18.** bought, **curios 19.** read, **minutes**
20. Did, make, **budget 21.** have, affected, **history 22.** baked, **pie**

Indirect Objects (P. 32)
The words in bold should be labeled DO, and the words underlined
twice should be labeled IO. **1.** threw, David, **ball 2.** gave, usher, **tickets**
3. handed, Chris, **prescription. 4.** sold, us, **set 5.** Have, written,
Andrea, **time 6.** paid, employee, **salary 7.** should teach, us, **wisdom**
8. sent, Amy, **letter 9.** show, us, **trick 10.** gave, cashier, **money**
11. gave, us, **story 12.** shows, visitors, **things 13.** gives, people, **hours**
14. give, group, **lecture 15.** has brought, us, **inventions 16.** take,
Sandra, **books 17.** gave, Joanne, **plants 18.** give, me, **drink 19.** gave,
flag, **name 20.** Will, give me, **instructions**

Independent and Subordinate Clauses (P. 33)
A. 1. We arrived late **2.** The play started **3.** We got one of the special
programs **4.** the audience applauded. **5.** we went for a walk. **6.** the
walk was enjoyable. **7.** I noticed the moon. **8.** it was shining brightly.
9. We walked along the lake **10.** it was almost midnight. **B. 1.** where
some trains travel at very fast speeds. **2.** that we saw **3.** that bears
his name. **4.** When you respect others, **5.** that was perfect for him.
6. who was elected without a run-off. **7.** that I purchased **8.** When I
awoke, **9.** who would control others **10.** that can stand the test of the
Sahara.

Adjective and Adverb Clauses (P. 34)
A. 1. adjective; whose bravery won many victories **2.** adjective; who
reads the most books **3.** adverb; because he hadn't set the alarm
4. adverb; when our team comes off the field **5.** adjective; that he
hears **6.** adjective; that we planned **B.** Sentences will vary.

Compound and Complex Sentences
(Pages 35–36) A. 1. CP **2.** CP **3.** CX **4.** CP **5.** CX **6.** CP **7.** CX
8. CX **9.** CP **10.** CP **11.** CP **12.** CX **13.** CX **14.** CX **15.** CP **16.** CP
17. CX **18.** CX **19.** CX **20.** CP **21.** CX **22.** CP **23.** CP **24.** CX
B. 1. [The streets are filled with cars], but [the sidewalks are empty.]
2. [Those apples are too sour to eat,] but [those pears are perfect.]
3. [She studies hard,] but [she saves some time to enjoy herself.]
4. [They lost track of time], so [they were late.] **5.** [Eric had not
studied,] so [he failed the test.] **6.** [Yesterday it rained all day,] but
[today the sun is shining.] **7.** [I set the alarm to get up early,] but [I
couldn't get up.] **8.** [They may sing and dance until dawn,] but [they
will be exhausted.] **9.** [My friend moved to Texas,] and [I will miss
her.] **10.** [They arrived at the theater early,] but [there was still a long
line.] **11.** [Lisa took her dog to the veterinarian,] but [his office was
closed.] **12.** [The black cat leaped,] but [fortunately it didn't catch the
bird.] **13.** [I found a baseball in the bushes,] and [I gave it to my
brother.] **14.** [We loaded the cart with groceries,] and [we went to the
checkout.] **15.** [The stadium was showered with lights,] but [the
stands were empty.] **16.** [The small child whimpered,] and [her
mother hugged her.] **17.** [The dark clouds rolled in,] and [then it began
to rain.] **C. 1.** that . . . backward. **2.** that . . . window **3.** that . . .
outside **4.** who . . . star **5.** who . . . artist **6.** that . . . microwave
7. who . . . music **8.** because . . . late **9.** When . . . arrives **10.** because
. . . leg **11.** When . . . podium **12.** If . . . talk **13.** that . . . city **14.** which
. . . red **15.** who . . . Georgia **16.** when . . . bat **17.** When . . . ball

Correcting Run-on Sentences (P. 37) Sentences may vary.
Expanding Sentences (P. 38) A. and B. Sentences will vary.

Unit 2 TEST (Pages 39–40)
1. B **2.** D **3.** C **4.** A **5.** B **6.** D **7.** A **8.** D **9.** D **10.** B **11.** C **12.** A
13. B **14.** A **15.** B **16.** B **17.** A **18.** B **19.** B **20.** B **21.** B **22.** A **23.** C
24. C **25.** A **26.** A **27.** C **28.** A **29.** B **30.** B **31.** B **32.** A **33.** C

Unit 3: Grammar and Usage
Common and Proper Nouns (P. 41)
A. Students should write P above the proper nouns in bold and C above
the underlined common nouns. **1. Maria**, sister **2. Honolulu**, city, capital,
Hawaii 3. Rainbow Natural Bridge, part, Utah **4. The Declaration of
Independence**, certificate, **United States 5. Abraham Lincoln, Edgar
Allan Poe, Frederic Chopin**, year **B. and C.** Answers will vary.

Concrete, Abstract, and Collective Nouns (P. 42)
[con=concrete; coll=collective; ab=abstract] **1.** ab **2.** ab **3.** coll **4.** ab
5. coll **6.** con **7.** coll **8.** coll **9.** con **10.** coll **11.** ab **12.** coll **13.** ab
14. con **15.** coll **16.** ab **17.** con **18.** coll **19.** con **20.** ab **21.** coll
22. coll **23.** con **24.** ab **25.** coll **26.** coll **27.** con **28.** ab **29.** coll
30. con **31.** coll **32.** ab **33.** coll **34.** con **35.** coll **36.** ab **37.** con
38. con **39.** ab **40.** con **41.** ab **42.** ab

Singular and Plural Nouns (Pages 43–44)
A. 1. counties **2.** ponies **3.** tomatoes **4.** banjos **5.** matches
6. windows **7.** centuries **8.** trenches **9.** bookcases **10.** videos
11. radios **12.** farms **13.** flies **14.** heroes **15.** dresses **16.** boots
17. desks **18.** daisies **B. 1.** mouthful **2.** proof **3.** 6 **4.** calf **5.** knife
6. Jones **7.** child **8.** goose **9.** wolf **10.** roof **11.** gentleman
12. editor-in-chief **13.** + **14.** cupful **15.** trout **16.** mouse
C. 1. boxes **2.** cities **3.** deer **4.** flashes **5.** coaches **6.** churches
7. potatoes **8.** e's **9.** O'Keefes **10.** fish **11.** scarves **12.** n's
13. radios **14.** oxen **15.** pilots **16.** 90's **17.** women **18.** i's

Possessive Nouns (P. 45)
1. Steve's **2.** mother's **3.** friends' **4.** woman's **5.** collector's
6. Rosa's; child's **7.** Warrens' **8.** vice-president's **9.** mayor's
10. Tony's **11.** women's **12.** family's **13.** day's **14.** lifeguards'
15. team's **16.** children's **17.** Juan's **18.** Jim's **19.** Calvin's
20. Lees' **21.** Mark's **22.** Frank's; Jean's **23.** neighbors'
24. Masons' **25.** States'

Appositives (P. 46)
Students should circle the words in bold. **1. Jan Matzeliger**, the . . .
machine, **2. Niagara Falls**, the . . . York, **3. Harvard**, the . . . States,
4. brother Jim **5. Diane Feinstein**, a . . . Francisco, **6. Sears Tower**,
the . . . world, **7. cousin** Liz **8. Leontyne Price**, the . . . singer,
9. ship the Mayflower **10. dog** Jasmine **11. Dr. Miller**, our . . .
physician, **12. swimmer** Mark Spitz **13. Fort Worth**, a . . . Texas,
14. Aunt Lee, my . . . sister, **15. Mr. Diddon**, coach . . . team,
16. Monticello, Jefferson's home, **17. inventor** Thomas Edison
18. Athens, the . . . Greece, **19. king** Montezuma **20. weevil**, a small
beetle, **21. Hoover Dam**, a . . . River, **22. Antares**, a . . . sun,
23. composer Mozart **24. copperhead**, one . . . States. **25. Mt.
McKinley**, a . . . mountain,

Verbs (P. 47)
1. is scattering; scattered; (have, had, has) scattered **2.** is expressing;
expressed; (have, had, has) expressed **3.** is painting; painted; (have,
had, has) painted **4.** is calling; called; (have, had, has) called **5.** is
cooking; cooked; (have, had, has) cooked **6.** is observing; observed;
(have, had, has) observed **7.** is looking; looked; (have, had, has)
looked **8.** is walking; walked; (have, had, has) walked **9.** is rambling;
rambled; (have, had, has) rambled **10.** is shouting; shouted; (have,
had, has) shouted **11.** is noticing; noticed; (have, had, has) noticed
12. is ordering; ordered; (have, had, has) ordered **13.** is gazing;
gazed; (have, had, has) gazed **14.** is borrowing; borrowed; (have,
had, has) borrowed **15.** is starting; started; (have, had, has) started
16. is working; worked; (have, had, has) worked

Verb Phrases (P. 48)
A. Students should circle the words in bold. **1. have** heard **2. was**
born, **has** become **3. may have** heard **4. had** grown **5. had** learned
6. was, interested, **had** heard **7. had** declared, **will** go, plant **8. had**
done, **had** moved **9. should**, do, asked **10. will** plant, was

11. could, remain **12. was** traveling, pushed **13.** called, **did**, have **14. would** sleep **B.** Sentences will vary.

Verb Tenses (P. 49)
1. brought; past **2.** know; present **3.** will close; future **4.** will continue; future **5.** has donated; present perfect **6.** had told; past perfect **7.** was; past **8.** sings; present **9.** will have paid; future perfect **10.** will have been; future perfect **11.** had been playing; past perfect **12.** have anchored; present perfect

Using Irregular Verbs (Pages 50–54)
A. 1. (is) doing; did; (has) done **2.** (is) coming; came; (has) come **3.** (is) eating; ate; (has) eaten **4.** (is) going; went; (has) gone **5.** (is) seeing; saw; (has) seen **6.** (is) taking; took; (has) taken **B. 1.** seen **2.** seen **3.** taking **4.** seen **5.** eaten **6.** gone **7.** going **8.** eaten **9.** gone **10.** taking **11.** did **12.** done **13.** taking **14.** come **15.** eaten **16.** seen **17.** came or come **18.** did **C. 1.** is beginning; began; has begun **2.** is drinking; drank; has drunk **3.** is driving; drove; has driven **4.** is giving; gave; has given **5.** is running; ran; has run **D. 1.** gave or is giving **2.** ran or are running **3.** begun **4.** began **5.** drunk **6.** driven **7.** given **8.** beginning **9.** run **10.** ran or is running **11.** began **12.** given **13.** beginning **14.** ran **15.** given **16.** gave **17.** begun **18.** drunk **19.** began **20.** running **E. 1.** is growing; grew; has grown **2.** is knowing; knew; has known **3.** is ringing; rang; has rung **4.** is singing; sang; has sung **5.** is speaking; spoke; has spoken **F. 1.** sung **2.** grew **3.** knew **4.** grown **5.** singing **6.** rung **7.** grown **8.** spoke **9.** rang **10.** spoken **11.** speaking **12.** sang **13.** known **14.** rang **15.** thrown **16.** grown **17.** known **18.** growing **19.** rang **20.** spoken **G. 1.** is blowing; blew; has blown **2.** is breaking; broke; has broken **3.** is choosing; chose; has chosen **4.** is drawing; drew; has drawn **5.** is flying; flew; has flown **H.** Answers may vary for numbers 2, 4, 7, and 10. Suggested: **1.** drawn **2.** blew **3.** flying **4.** chose **5.** chosen **6.** blown **7.** broke **8.** broken **9.** choosing **10.** drew **11.** broken **12.** broke **13.** chosen **14.** broke **15.** froze **16.** chosen **17.** broke **18.** drawn **19.** breaking **20.** drawn **I. 1.** is becoming; became; has become **2.** is falling; fell; has fallen **3.** is riding; rode; has ridden **4.** is rising; rose; has risen **5.** is stealing; stole; has stolen **6.** is showing; showed; has shown **7.** is sinking; sank; has sunk **8.** is swimming; swam; has swum **9.** is tearing; tore; has torn **10.** is wearing; wore; has worn **J. 1.** ridden **2.** risen **3.** wore **4.** stolen **5.** riding **6.** swimming **7.** tore **8.** sank **9.** stolen **10.** ridden **11.** worn **12.** worn **13.** rose **14.** risen **15.** fallen

Mood (P. 55)
[ind=indicative; sub=subjunctive; imp=imperative] **1.** imp **2.** ind **3.** sub **4.** imp **5.** ind **6.** ind **7.** ind **8.** sub **9.** imp **10.** sub **11.** imp **12.** imp **13.** ind **14.** sub **15.** ind **16.** ind **17.** sub **18.** imp **19.** sub

Transitive and Intransitive Verbs (Pages 56–57)
[T=transitive; I=intransitive] **A. 1.** walked; I **2.** is; I **3.** Move; T **4.** listened; I **5.** wore; T **6.** built; T **7.** is; I **8.** lives; I **9.** elected; T **10.** paid; T **11.** send; T **12.** is; I **13.** drew; T **14.** study; I **15.** cried; I **16.** made; T **17.** ran; I **18.** learned; T **19.** barked; I **20.** bring; T **21.** baked; T **B. 1.** signed; T **2.** repaired; T **3.** shipped; T **4.** may cause; T **5.** was; I **6.** has; T **7.** Explain; T **8.** whistled; I **9.** blocked; T **10.** have dropped; I **11.** change; T **12.** attracts; T **13.** was; I **14.** has; T **15.** invented; T **16.** cooked; T **17.** discovered; T **18.** traveled; I **19.** composed; T **20.** was; I **21.** destroyed; T **22.** exercises; I **23.** talked; I **24.** Have seen; T **25.** cause; T **26.** is studying; I **27.** bought; T

Active and Passive Voice (P. 58)
[A=active; P=passive] **1.** was invented; P **2.** hit; A **3.** was rung; P **4.** was thrown; P **5.** has bought; A **6.** was announced; P **7.** blamed; A **8.** were selected; P **9.** typed; A **10.** stated; A **11.** flopped; A **12.** were written; P **13.** gave; A **14.** held; A **15.** has bought; A **16.** was broken; P **17.** shook; A **18.** was carried; P **19.** was given; P **20.** wrote; A

Gerunds (P. 59)
1. living **2.** fighting **3.** Landing **4.** Climbing **5.** moaning **6.** barking **7.** Keeping **8.** hanging **9.** Laughing **10.** Being **11.** Making **12.** Winning **13.** pitching **14.** eating **15.** Playing **16.** Planning **17.** packing **18.** howling **19.** doing **20.** living **21.** planting; hunting

fishing **22.** writing **23.** skating **24.** boating **25.** Pressing **26.** mapping **27.** Swimming **28.** driving

Infinitives (P. 60)
1. to go **2.** to see **3.** to serve **4.** To shoot **5.** to walk **6.** to stand; to sit; to walk; to dance **7.** to use; to make **8.** to get **9.** to make **10.** to clean **11.** to be **12.** to travel **13.** to play **14.** to rise **15.** to see **16.** to enter **17.** to mail **18.** To cook **19.** to meet **20.** to speak **21.** to exhibit **22.** To succeed **23.** to see **24.** to eat **25.** to see **26.** to have; to be **27.** to receive **28.** To score **29.** to go **30.** to paint

Participles (P. 61)
1. running **2.** showing **3.** scampering **4.** hidden **5.** advancing **6.** Biting **7.** falling **8.** whispering **9.** preparing **10.** enjoying **11.** produced **12.** burdened **13.** thinking **14.** injured **15.** expanding **16.** fanned **17.** shoving **18.** frozen **19.** playing **20.** cleaned **21.** Teasing **22.** lifting **23.** chirping **24.** surviving **25.** dedicated **26.** Homing **27.** whistling **28.** Ironed **29.** standing **30.** loving

Using Lie/Lay (P. 62)
A. 1. lies **2.** Lay **3.** lying **4.** lie **5.** laid **6.** laid **7.** lain **8.** lie **9.** laid **10.** lies **11.** lain **12.** lay **13.** lies **B.** Sentences will vary.

Using Sit/Set and Learn/Teach (P. 63)
1. set **2.** teaching **3.** learn **4.** sit **5.** sitting **6.** teach **7.** sit **8.** sat **9.** teach **10.** sit **11.** teach; learn **12.** sat **13.** set **14.** teach **15.** set **16.** taught **17.** teach **18.** sit **19.** taught **20.** taught **21.** set **22.** set **23.** teaching **24.** sitting

Pronouns (P. 64)
1. you; my **2.** you; me; I; them **3.** you; me; our **4.** I; you **5.** We; him **6.** me **7.** We; they; us **8.** She; me **9.** She; you; me; her **10.** We; them **11.** we; our **12.** He; their **13.** She; my **14.** They; us; them **15.** she **16.** he; you **17.** She; us **18.** I **19.** your **20.** me **21.** you; our **22.** I; you; my; you; it **23.** I; him; my; we; her **24.** they; us; their **25.** Your; your **26.** us; her; our

Using Its and It's (P. 65)
A. 1. its **2.** It's **3.** it's **4.** It's **5.** it's **6.** It's **7.** It's **8.** It's; its **9.** its **10.** It's **11.** it's **12.** its **13.** its **14.** it's **15.** its **16.** It's **17.** its **18.** its **19.** it's **20.** its **B. and C.** Sentences will vary.

Demonstrative and Indefinite Pronouns (P. 66)
A. 1. Those **2.** That **3.** these **4.** This; that **5.** those **6.** that **7.** This **8.** these **9.** These **10.** this **11.** those **12.** this **13.** those **14.** These **15.** that **16.** that **B. 1.** Both **2.** each **3.** Several **4.** some **5.** Everyone **6.** someone **7.** Some **8.** each **9.** anyone **10.** someone **11.** Both **12.** One **13.** Each **14.** Some **15.** someone **16.** Everybody

Antecedents (P. 67)
Students should circle the words in bold. **1. Everyone**; his or her **2. Each**; his or her **3. Sophia**; her **4. I**; my **5. members**; their **6. women**; their **7. Someone**; her or his **8. each**; his or her **9. Joanne**; her **10. woman**; her **11. anyone**; his or her **12. student**; his or her **13. I**; my **14. woman**; her **15. one**; his or her **16. Joseph**; his **17. man**; his **18. waiters**; their **19. student**; his or her **20. person**; her or his **21. man**; his **22. woman**; her **23. Jeff and Tom**; their **24. Cliff**; he **25. bird**; its **26. Mark**; his

Relative Pronouns (P. 68)
Students should circle the words in bold. **1. letter;** that **2. Karen;** who **3. Robert Burns;** who **4. Sylvia;** who **5. shop;** that **6. farmhouse;** that **7. pearl;** that **8. bridge;** which **9. animal;** that **10. regions;** that **11. turkey;** that **12. story;** which **13. person;** whom **14. hamburgers;** that **15. food;** that **16. painting;** that **17. sweater;** that **18. one;** whom **19. money;** that **20. person;** who **21. animal;** that **22. guests;** whom **23. file;** which **24. artist;** whose **25. attraction;** that **26. writer;** whom

Using Who/Whom (P. 69)
1. Who **2.** Who **3.** Whom **4.** Who **5.** Who **6.** Who **7.** whom **8.** whom **9.** Who **10.** whom **11.** Whom **12.** Whom **13.** whom **14.** Who **15.** Whom **16.** whom **17.** whom **18.** Whom **19.** Who **20.** Whom **21.** Who

Using Pronouns (P. 70)
1. I **2.** He; I **3.** that **4.** he; she **5.** me **6.** who **7.** Whom **8.** me **9.** whom **10.** me **11.** whom **12.** her; me **13.** she; him **14.** who **15.** those **16.** she **17.** me **18.** his or her **19.** me **20.** Those **21.** me

22. him 23. These 24. he 25. he 26. Those 27. me 28. he
29. whom 30. their 31. Who 32. she 33. his or her 34. who

Adjectives (Pages 71–72)

A. 1. The; old; fabulous; Greek 2. The; little; a; affectionate 3. The; weary; the; soft; green 4. The; a; magnificent; vivid 5. Every; good; good; good 6. Every; the; the; famous 7. Fleecy; white 8. every; lofty 9. many; clear; bright 10. a 11. The; beautiful; memorial; the; main; the; city 12. Cautious; dangerous 13. fertile; extensive; valuable; a; great 14. a; massive; a; broad; deep; large; black 15. The; the; a; dreary 16. a; daily 17. The; main; stately 18. a; friendly 19. The; second; the; fourth; broken 20. The; bright; colorful; the; a; wonderful 21. The; old; dusty; the 22. Yellow; green; the; curious 23. The; steaming; blueberry; the 24. An; elegant; the; black 25. the; chirping; baby 26. The; the; first B. Sentences will vary. 1. Puerto Rican 2. Irish 3. South American 4. British 5. French 6. Roman 7. Canadian 8. English 9. Russian C. and D. Adjectives will vary.

Demonstrative Adjectives (P. 73)

1. those 2. those 3. these 4. those 5. These 6. that 7. this 8. Those 9. those 10. that 11. those 12. these 13. Those 14. Those 15. that 16. these 17. this 18. Those 19. that 20. those 21. this 22. Those 23. these 24. This 25. that

Comparing with Adjectives (P. 74)

A. 1. gentler; gentlest 2. more helpful; most helpful 3. more difficult; most difficult 4. more troublesome; most troublesome 5. higher; highest 6. more delicious; most delicious 7. more intelligent; most intelligent 8. softer; softest B. 1. most difficult 2. lovelier 3. more agreeable

Adverbs (P. 75)

1. rapidly 2. very 3. Slowly; surely 4. Afterward; soundly 5. carefully; thoroughly 6. gracefully 7. Slowly; steadily 8. too; rapidly 9. always; stylishly; neatly 10. quickly; abruptly 11. seriously 12. extremely; slowly; away 13. Always; correctly; clearly 14. rapidly 15. very; quietly 16. patiently; carefully 17. everywhere 18. too; quickly 19. gently 20. here; there; everywhere 21. here; immediately 22. gaily; everywhere 23. Slowly 24. Overhead; brightly 25. thoroughly 26. speedily 27. Carefully 28. quite 29. too

Comparing with Adverbs (P. 76)

A. 1. faster; fastest 2. more carefully; most carefully 3. more quietly; most quietly 4. slower; slowest 5. more frequently; most frequently 6. more proudly; most proudly 7. more evenly; most evenly 8. longer; longest B. 1. more seriously 2. highest 3. more thoroughly 4. worst 5. more diligently 6. best

Using Adjectives and Adverbs (P. 77)

1. carefully 2. calm 3. furiously 4. patiently 5. cheerfully 6. well 7. promptly 8. respectfully 9. happy 10. legibly 11. slowly 12. happily 13. surely 14. well 15. easily 16. loudly 17. brightly 18. well 19. quickly 20. suddenly 21. cautiously 22. accurately 23. furiously 24. new 25. steadily 26. beautiful 27. courteously 28. well 29. well 30. really 31. foolishly 32. foolish 33. loudly 34. rapidly

Prepositions and Prepositional Phrases

(Pages 78–79) Students should circle the words in bold. 1. **in** 1847 2. **for** creating the beloved detective Sherlock Holmes 3. **in** the United States; **in** 1884 4. **of** the United States; **in** Kansas 5. **for** miners; **by** Sir Humphrey Davy; **in** 1816 6. **of** North Borneo; **in** houses; **on** stilts; **in** the Brunei River 7. **by** the magician's tricks 8. **in** Canada 9. **in** New York City; **in** 1900 10. **in** the United States; **in** Jamestown; **in** 1619 11. **in** the world; **in** New York; **in** 1832 12. **of** the telephone; **in** Scotland 13. **of** the printing press 14. **of** the giant skyscrapers; **before** us 15. **in** the waves 16. **by** Thomas Jefferson 17. **upon** the quiet valley 18. **to** sleep; **by** the patter; **of** the rain 19. **beneath** the tree 20. **in** the middle; **of** the road 21. **across** the yard; **around** the tree 22. **across** the brook 23. **of** our country; **in** 1790 24. **of** violets; **into** perfume 25. **of** a person; **of** blood; **in** one minute 26. **in** 1836 27. **of** the secrets; **of** success; **of** leisure time 28. **at** this hotel 29. **in** Washington, D.C. 30. **of** iron ore; **near** the western end; **of** the Great Lakes 31. **across** this stream; **by** the recent storm 32. **of** cattle; **on** these plains 33. **in** football; **by** a team; **from** Georgia University; **in** 1896 34. **in** Chicago 35. **of** a century ago; **by** stagecoach 36. **of** Delhi; **in** India; **to** the

skill; **of** its builders 37. **of** the evening; **by** the rumbling; **of** thunder 38. **in** a tree 39. **on** a sand dune; **in** North Carolina; **in** 1903 40. **in** Richmond; **in** 1885 41. **of** rusty nails; **in** the corner; **of** the garage 42. **near** the edge; **of** that steep cliff 43. **with** a deep snow 44. **in** the accident; **on** the expressway 45. **of** geography; **about** the layout; **of** other lands 46. **of** smoke; **from** the chimney; **of** the cabin 47. **In** the distance; **of** the snow-capped peak 48. **upon** the shelf 49. **At** one time; **of** the United States 50. **between** the goal posts 51. **of** the secretary; **at** the beginning; **of** the meeting 52. **of** cheering fans; **at** the entrance 53. **toward** the ground 54. **beneath** this huge tree 55. **In** the glow; **of** the fading light; **along** the road 56. **near** the new mall 57. **in** the card catalog; **in** the library 58. **through** the halls; **of** the mansion 59. **for** next year

Conjunctions (P. 80)

1. and 2. whereas 3. since 4. but 5. not only; but also 6. Neither; nor 7. and 8. Neither; nor 9. neither; nor 10. and 11. Either; or 12. and 13. Neither; nor 14. Although 15. when 16. since 17. while 18. Unless; before 19. although 20. Both; and 21. both; and 22. Unless 23. Neither; nor 24. while 25. when 26. Either; or 27. because

Double Negatives (P. 81)

1. anything 2. anything 3. any 4. anything 5. any 6. any 7. anyone 8. any 9. any 10. any 11. anything 12. anything 13. any 14. any 15. anybody 16. any 17. any 18. anything 19. any 20. any 21. anything 22. any 23. any 24. any 25. any 26. anyone 27. anybody 28. anyone 29. any

Unit 3 TEST (Pages 82–83)

1. B 2. C 3. C 4. A 5. B 6. A 7. C 8. B 9. B 10. C 11. A 12. A 13. D 14. B 15. A 16. C 17. B 18. A 19. C 20. B 21. C 22. A 23. C 24. A 25. A 26. A 27. B 28. A 29. B 30. C 31. B 32. B 33. B 34. A 35. C 36. D 37. B 38. C 39. B 40. B

Unit 4: Capitalization and Punctuation

Using Capital Letters (Pages 84–85)

Students should circle and capitalize the first letter in each of the following words. A. 1. Henry; Wadsworth; Longfellow; America; Evangeline; The; Courtship; Miles; Standish 2. The; Midnight; Ride; Paul; Revere; Longfellow's 3. British; *Titanic*; England; United; States 4. The; American; George; Wythe 5. He; Thomas; Jefferson; James; Monroe 6. Mississippi; River; Vicksburg; Mississippi; New; Orleans; Louisiana 7. What; Amelia 8. Robert; I 9. Vikings; Norway; Sweden; Denmark 10. The; The; Battle Hymn; Republic; Julia; Ward; Howe 11. James; Nelson; Chicago; Illinois 12. He; Have 13. President; United; States; White; House 14. Hopi 15. Sequoia; National; Park; Sierra; Nevada; Mountains; California B. 1. Mayor; Jones; Senator; Small 2. Dr.; Fox 3. Ms.; Hilary; Johnson 4. Judge; Randall 5. Gov.; Dickson 6. Senator; Christopher; Larson 7. Supt.; Adams 8. Miss; Alden; 9. Dr.; Tabor 10. Mr.; William; Benton C. 1. Maj.; Hanson 2. W.; Charles; St. 3. Orlando; FL 4. Maple Ave.; Sunset; St. 5. Mon.; September 6. Gen.; T.J.; Quint 7. Memphis; TN 8. Col.; Kravitz; Dover; NH 9. Falmouth; Harbor; Dover; NH

Using End Punctuation (Pages 86–87)

A. 1. ? 2. . 3. ? 4. . 5. . 6. ? 7. . 8. . 9. ? 10. ? 11. ? 12. . 13. . 14. ? B. Line 1. ? Line 3. . Line 4. . Line 5. . ; ? Line 6. . ; . Line 7. . ; . Line 8. . Line 9. . Line 10. . ; . Line 11. . Line 12. ? Line 13. . Line 14. . ; . C. 1. . or ! 2. . 3. . 4. ! ; ! or . 5. . 6. . 7. ! ; ! or . 8. ! 9. . 10. . 11. ! 12. ! ; ! 13. ! 14. . 15. . D. Line 2. ? ; . or ! Line 3. . Line 4. . or ! ; . or ! Line 5. . Line 6. . Line 7. ? ; . Line 8. . Line 9. . ; . Line 10. ? Line 11. . ; . Line 12. . Line 13. . . or ! ; ?

Using Commas (Pages 88–89)

A. 1. Anita, Travis, 2. seats, 3. game, 4. Fergas, 5. good, 6. match, clapped, cheered, 7. matches, 8. autographs, 9. name, ball, 10. much, Travis, José, 11. men's, women's, 12. tournament, B. 1. A.M., 2. asked, 3. me, 4. said, 5. binoculars, Anita, C. 1. Perillo, nutritionist, 2. Students, 3. Yes, 4. First, 5. Yes, 6. Perillo, 7. Okay, 8. serving, Emilio, 9. Dave, runner, 10. Class, D. Line 1. neighbor, Patrick, Patrick, Line 2. Well, peaches, apricots, Line 3. pears, plums, variety, Line 4. son, Jonathon, Oh,